# RUTH
## A MODERN COMMENTARY

LEONARD S. KRAVITZ
and
KERRY M. OLITZKY

URJ PRESS
NEW YORK, NEW YORK

Library of Congress Cataloging-in-Publication Data

Kravitz, Leonard S.
  Ruth : a modern commentary / by Leonard S. Kravitz and Kerry M. Olitzky.
    p. cm.
  ISBN 0-8074-0849-2 (pbk. : alk. paper)   1. Bible. O.T. Ruth–Commentaries.
I. Olitzky, Kerry M.   II. Title.

BS1315.53K73 2005
222'.35077–dc22

2005042052

Typesetting: El Ot Pre Press & Computing Ltd., Tel Aviv
This book is printed on acid-free paper.
Copyright © 2005 by URJ Press
Manufactured in the United States of America
10  9  8  7  6  5  4  3  2  1

*To Hanna for everything*
*LSK*

*To honor the memory of Suse Rosenstock, z"l*
*KMO*

Dedicated to the memory of Naomi and her disciple,
Mildred Brenner Glickman,
whose wisdom and love in trying times enabled any choice
to be imbued with holiness.

May all who come to Judaism be met with such kindness.
"The highest wisdom is kindness"

# Contents

# *Permissions*

# *Acknowledgments*

Even as our lives take us to different places, we are grateful for the gift of Torah, which has a uniquely spiritual way of keeping us together as it transcends both time and space.

We want to acknowledge the teachings of Rabbi Jack Reimer, whose insights on the Book of Ruth helped to frame an understanding of some of the introductory material to this volume.

We thank former and current students at Hebrew Union College–Jewish Institute of Religion, who allowed us to share our insights with them, and we thank our colleagues at HUC-JIR and at the Jewish Outreach Institute, who support our efforts to teach Torah to others. We also thank the many people who have joined with the Jewish Outreach Institute and its efforts to create a more inclusive Jewish community.

We thank Rabbi Hara Person and those at the URJ Press, including Debra Hirsch Corman, Michael Goldberg, Ron Ghatan, Debbie Fellman, Dahlia Schoenberg, and Victor Ney, who continue to sustain our long-term project of providing informed access in order to gain mastery of individual books in our sacred tradition.

We are also mindful of all of those Jews-by-choice who look to the Book of Ruth for insight and guidance. To all those who have cast their lot with the Jewish people, we say: *B'ruchim habaim*—a blessed welcome.

*Leonard S. Kravitz*
*Kerry (Shia) Olitzky*
*Chanukah 5763*

*Editor's Note on the Hebrew Text:*

Tradition has preserved textual variants in the Hebrew Bible by noting instances when a word was written one way, but pronounced a different way. In this volume, the written version, called the *ketiv*, appears in smaller print and without vowels, while the spoken version, or *keri*, appears as part of the regular Hebrew text.

# Introduction

Set in the time of the Judges, Ruth is first of all a book of romance, cast in a pastoral setting. Most people think of the Book of Ruth as an intellectual biography of the biblical character of Ruth, paying less attention to Naomi, whose own traumatic life introduces the book. But it is Naomi who learns the lessons of life and whose own character and perseverance offer us a model by which to live. Today, many relate the Book of Ruth to the positive experience of contemporary Jews-by-choice, who have embraced Judaism in their own lives, as well as those who have chosen to cast their lot with the Jewish people by living in its midst without the benefit of conversion. We understand the essence of this commitment in Ruth's own awe-inspiring words: "Don't beg me to leave you or to keep from following you, because wherever you go, I will go. Wherever you stay, I will stay. Your people will be my people. And your God will be my God" (1:16). It is important to note, however, that while Naomi may not have been initially supportive of her sons' marriages to non-Israelite women, the mutually supportive and accepting relationship that developed between Naomi and Ruth is perhaps unparalleled in the Bible. But it was not until the deaths of her sons that Naomi was able to open her heart and welcome Ruth.

The Book of Ruth includes four chapters and is part of the third section of the Bible called Writings (*K'tuvim* in Hebrew). It is also part of a subsection, what is known as the *Chameish M'gillot* (Five Scrolls). The reading of each scroll is assigned to a holiday. Ruth is read during Shavuot, probably because of the grain harvest that figures prominently in both the book and the holiday. Thus it becomes a book of personal harvest, as well. Since Shavuot marks the giving of the Torah to the Jewish people—and their acceptance of it—it is appropriate to link Ruth to the holiday. More than anything else, Jews-by-choice are asked to accept the Torah in principle and its particulars. In addition, since the Sinai experience is part of the historical memory of the Jewish people, those new to Judaism take on the memory of this experience as their own.

The Book of Ruth contains numerous themes and lessons that can be applied to contemporary life. It presents readers with a sense of the difficulties of living in the Land of Israel, as well as the challenges of living outside the Land. Through its use of central women characters, Ruth suggests a variety of roles for women; in so doing, it raises questions concerning their legal status and abilities. Furthermore, it deals frankly with intermarriage. This makes Ruth's own acceptance of Judaism—and her role as the progenitor of King David and the beginning of the messianic lineage (Ruth 4:13–22)—even more dramatic, since, as a Moabite, she is a member of a tribe that, according to the Torah, was to be prohibited from entering the Jewish community (Deuteronomy 23:4).

The Book of Ruth reflects the reality of Jews who had to leave the Land of Israel for economic reasons. They settled where they could do business. As a result, they married people who were part of the society in which they settled. While the author of Ruth does not blame Elimelech and his sons for leaving the Land due to famine, later commentators on the book certainly did. Nor does the author blame the men for "marrying out," since they settled in a foreign land. Instead, Naomi is touched by the kindness of her Moabite daughters-in-law, especially following the deaths of her sons, their husbands. The lack of hostility expressed by Naomi takes most modern Jewish readers by surprise.

The Book of Ruth begins by introducing readers to Naomi, along with her husband and two sons. Naomi quickly encounters a series of life challenges, one after another. With each event Naomi is thrown into the pit of despair, even as she tries to raise herself up from the preceding event. First Naomi experiences a severe famine that depletes her resources. She promptly learns the fragile nature of personal wealth. Next Naomi has to leave home and everything behind in order to escape that famine. As a result, she is forced to endure personal exile in Moab. After living there for ten years, her husband dies, and so she must raise her two sons by herself. Both her children then marry local Moabite women and subsequently die.

Like Job, Naomi loses everything in life that has given her any meaning, direction, or purpose. She has lost her personal identity. She feels isolated, bewildered, confused. Over and over, her voice of despair cries out to the heavens from the pages of the Bible.

So Naomi returns destitute to Bethlehem. Unable to dissuade Ruth from coming with her, Naomi is followed by her Moabite daughter-in-law. Not only does Naomi embrace Ruth—the woman who was an outsider—but it is Ruth who helps Naomi slowly become whole once again. The stranger, the one who has come the furthest distance, becomes the most intimate, the one who is able to make the most impact on Naomi—once Naomi opens herself up to all that Ruth has to offer.

Since Jews in the ancient world, as early as Abraham, were involved with trade throughout the Fertile Crescent, an area bordered by the Tigris and Euphrates Rivers, they often traveled outside of the Land of Israel. Where individuals came to do business, communities followed, a phenomenon that was replicated around the world throughout Jewish history. City life created new possibilities for interaction and the development of relationships with others. The temptation of exogamous marriage presented itself frequently, as it does today. As a result, the question of the identity of children from such marriages was raised. The Book of Ruth argues that not only do such marriages occur (as with Mahlon and Chilion), but they can also have positive outcomes (as with Boaz).

The writer of this biblical book clearly makes Ruth the hero of the story, fully aware that to do so goes against the teachings of Deuteronomy, which states "An Ammonite or Moabite shall not enter the congregation of *Adonai*, even into the tenth generation shall they not enter the congregation of *Adonai* forever" (Deuteronomy 23:4). Perhaps it was social conditions that prompted the position. Or perhaps the author felt that the notion of promoting an inclusive Jewish community transcended the specific direction of the Torah text.

Not only does the book present a realistic view of intermarriage, it also reveals a surprising amount of information concerning sexual desire and marriage. It may challenge our contemporary sensibilities about gender roles and sexuality, but Naomi frankly instructs Ruth in the art of seduction. She tells her to wash, put on perfume, wait until Boaz has eaten and drunk and has lain down in the field, and then lie down with him. It may be astonishing to read in the Bible that an older woman advises a younger woman, her former daughter-in-law, to "uncover" a man's feet, a euphemism for sexual intercourse. The Bible thus portrays Naomi and Ruth as initiators of sexual activity. However, the rabbinic interpretation of the text shifts its plain meaning, arguing that nothing happened or could have happened, given the necessary modesty of both women.

The Book of Ruth also depicts an account of inheritance that differs from what is described in the Torah or what later developed in the interpretation of the book by the Rabbis. It conflates the role of the *go-eil*, the person bound to redeem a relative's land and debt bondage (Leviticus 25:33, 25:48) with the role of the *yibum*, the one bound to marry his brother's childless widow and have children with her so that the name of his brother is not "wiped out" (Genesis 38:8; Deuteronomy 25:5–6). According to the Book of Ruth, the *go-eil* is responsible for both. However, it is clear from the Book of Ruth that the relationship among family members is quite distant. Neither Boaz nor the man he replaces is a close relative. While the text does not offer a reason why the nearest relative does not acquire the property of Naomi and Ruth, it is made clear that the property belongs to the two women. Thus, the Book of Ruth raises a series of technical problems: Why does the inheritance of Naomi and Ruth's property entail the acquisition of Ruth? Why did the relatives of Elimelech, Mahlon, and Chilion not already gain title to the property? And if an act of redemption was required, why did the nearest relative refrain from acting on his responsibility? While the possible resolution to these challenges will be dealt with in this translation and commentary, it may be a simple literary device to allow for the entry of Boaz and his role as hero.

In this volume, we use the lens of three different commentators through which to view the text: the *Targum* (a ca. fifth-century Aramaic translation, interpretation, and commentary of the Hebrew text); Rashi (1040–1105); and Abraham ibn Ezra (1092–1167). Since the *Targum* and Rashi reflect the notions of Rabbinic Judaism, their interpretations share much in common. The comments made by Ibn Ezra, on the other hand, reflect the impact of philosophy on Judaism. The *Targum* provides the reader with a primer on Rabbinic Judaism through the guise of a commentary. Since it translated the Hebrew text into Aramaic, the *lingua franca* of the community, it took a great deal of liberties in its translation and interpretation. It used the regular reading of the text as an educational opportunity to explain the requirements of Rabbinic Judaism to the community and what was required of its members. On occasion, we also take guidance from the *Biblia Hebraica*, a familiar critical edition of the Bible edited by Kittel. Finally, we take some direction from the critical scholarly work of Koehler-Baumgartner and regularly consult their *Lexicon* as a reference.

The rabbinic interpretation of Ruth in the *Targum* presents the reader with additional challenges to resolve and takes the story to places where it may never have been intended to go. At the beginning of the story, Ruth offers her oft-repeated statement of loyalty, cited above. The *Targum* reads this as an expression of Ruth's intent to convert to Judaism and frames it as responses to a series of questions put by Naomi, mimicking those later asked of converts by the *beit din* as part of the conversion process. For example, the *Targum* reads Ruth's statement, "Wherever you go [literally, 'walk'], I will go [literally 'walk']" (1:16), as a response to Naomi's asking, "Do you know that in keeping the Sabbath and Festivals you may not walk more than 2,000 cubits?"

In their commentaries, the Rabbis often read between the lines of the Book of Ruth as a way to engage in their somewhat esoteric world of Jewish legal argument. An example can be found at the conclusion of Ruth's well-known speech in 1:16–17. The *Targum* has Naomi ask Ruth, "Do you know that we have four methods of judicial execution: stoning, burning, beheading, and hanging on the gallows?" Ruth answers, "As you die, will I die." The *Targum* takes the rules from the Mishnah and supplies it as part of Ruth's conversation with Naomi. In other words, if she is going to join the Jewish people, these are the kinds of regulations she must understand. It is interesting that the *Mishnah Sanhedrin* (5:1) text includes three of the methods of execution as they are articulated in the commentary. However, the fourth differs. In the Mishnah, strangling is listed instead of hanging. The *Targum*'s commentator was probably using a variant manuscript edition of the Mishnah, something that is not uncommon in rabbinic commentaries, or combined the reading from two different sources. What is meant by strangling is clarified later in the Mishnah: the punishment of strangling did not involve hanging on a gallows (*Mishnah Sanhedrin* 7:3). Apparently, instead two men pulled on a rope wrapped around the condemned's neck until death. What is important in all this is that the *Targum* uses this opportunity to stress the importance of rabbinic law, especially for a convert to Judaism. Its message is that it is not only the Bible that is the primary source of Jewish law, and that converts should become well versed in rabbinic law.

While these items may seem irrelevant to an understanding of Ruth or an application for our lives, they help us determine the dating of the Mishnah and its dissemination. A current understanding of the laws regarding levirate marriage requires the individual to remove a sandal during this ritual. Since the text suggests that Boaz removes a sleeve, it means that the text most likely predates the codified and accepted version of the Mishnah. Such texts also assist us in the dating of the *Targum* and provide evidence that separate Jewish legal streams coexisted until one was given primacy when it was formed into the Mishnah and accepted as the standard version of the Oral Law. Perhaps the writer of the *Targum* knew the Mishnah and chose to follow a different legal tradition. If this is the case, then there was no central halachic authority during the period of the time when the *Targum* was prepared.

Since Ruth becomes the paradigm for conversion to Judaism, the Book of Ruth is championed by many Jews-by-choice in the community and has become the preferred text of many programs that reach out to non-Jews. This book allows those who would like to come close to Judaism to do so by way of studying sacred text, fully conscious that it is the text study that is the touchstone of Jewish spiritual practice and simultaneously affirms their place in the community.

# CHAPTER ONE

א:א וַיְהִי בִּימֵי שְׁפֹט הַשֹּׁפְטִים וַיְהִי רָעָב בָּאָרֶץ וַיֵּלֶךְ אִישׁ מִבֵּית לֶחֶם
יְהוּדָה לָגוּר בִּשְׂדֵי מוֹאָב הוּא וְאִשְׁתּוֹ וּשְׁנֵי בָנָיו:

**1:1** IN THE DAYS WHEN THE JUDGES GOVERNED, THERE
WAS A FAMINE IN THE LAND. SO A MAN FROM [THE
CITY OF] BETHLEHEM IN [THE LAND OF] JUDAH WENT
TO DWELL IN THE COUNTRY OF MOAB, TOGETHER
WITH HIS SPOUSE AND TWO SONS.

Although the story is placed in the period of the judges, it is clear that it was written
much later. This can be ascertained from the statement in 4:7, ''This used to be the
practice in Israel: to establish an act of redemption or exchange...,'' implying that
the reader would otherwise not know about the use of a sandal as a marker of the
transfer of title. In this statement, the author indicates the difference in time between
when events ostensibly occurred and when they were written down.

Moab is the nonspeaking but eloquent character of this story. As a place, Moab
is the stage upon which the initial, crucial action in the story takes place. Moab is
also the particular people of the hero of the story, Ruth. Although the Torah denigrates
the origins of the people as the products of incest (Genesis 19:37) and prohibits a
Moabite from entering the Jewish people (Deuteronomy 23:4), elsewhere we find
that David found shelter among the people of Moab when he fled from Saul
(I Samuel 22:3–4). The Book of Ruth presents a story of a Moabite woman entering
the Land of Israel with her mother-in-law, Naomi. Not only is she accepted into
the House of Israel, she becomes the progenitor of King David and, as a result, the
progenitor of the Messiah. Hence, it is a Moabite who will bring on the Messiah
even though the Torah claims elsewhere that Moabites cannot become part of the
Jewish people.

Whether the author lived prior to, during, or after the Babylonian exile, it seems
clear that the kinds of interaction with non-Jews assumed by this book reflect city life
rather than country living. It implicitly assumes the life of the city merchant, rather
than the life of the shepherd or farmer.

Throughout the Book of Judges, eighteen people named as judges acted as tribal
chiefs rather than magistrates. We have elected to retain the traditional translation of
*shoftim* as ''judges.'' However, in order to clarify their role, we have translated *sh'fot*

1

*hashoftim* as "the judges governed," taking into consideration the ambiguity of the two Hebrew words. The Hebrew could mean either "the judges did the judging" or "the judges were judged." The latter understanding serves the purposes of theodicy: famine came upon the Land because of human action, rather than divine responsibility. Famine was the punishment for the corruption of the judges.

The *Targum* begins by placing the famine in a list of ten famines that occurred or will occur from the time the world was created until the time of the coming of the Messiah. The first five occurred during the lives of (1) Adam, (2) Lamech, (3) Abraham, (4) Isaac, and (5) Jacob. The sixth, the famine discussed in the Book of Ruth, emerged during the time of Boaz. The seventh famine occurred during David's life, the eighth while Elijah was alive, and the ninth in Elisha's lifetime. The last famine mentioned in the *Targum* is one that has not yet taken place. This final famine will not be due to a lack of food or water. Rather, it will result from a lack of the hearing of the word of divine prophecy.

Rashi explains that the verse is a reference to what happened prior to the reign of Saul when the generations were governed by the judges. Rashi also refers to the rabbinic claim that one of the last judges—whose name was Ibzan (Judges 12:8)—was actually Boaz.

Abraham ibn Ezra notes that the term *sh'fot hashoftim* means that God judged the judges because it was their fault that famine came to the Land of Israel. According to the midrash, they proclaimed laws that they themselves did not keep (*Ruth Rabbah* 1:1). However, he acknowledges that others explain the term simply as "the judges judged," allowing for other possible interpretations.

א:ב וְשֵׁם הָאִישׁ אֱלִימֶלֶךְ וְשֵׁם אִשְׁתּוֹ נָעֳמִי וְשֵׁם שְׁנֵי־בָנָיו מַחְלוֹן
וְכִלְיוֹן אֶפְרָתִים מִבֵּית לֶחֶם יְהוּדָה וַיָּבֹאוּ שְׂדֵי־מוֹאָב וַיִּהְיוּ־שָׁם:

**1:2** THE MAN'S NAME WAS ELIMELECH. HIS SPOUSE'S NAME
WAS NAOMI. AND THE NAMES OF HIS TWO SONS WERE
MAHLON AND CHILION. THEY WERE EPHRATITES OF
BETHLEHEM IN JUDAH. THEY CAME TO THE LAND OF
MOAB AND STAYED THERE.

Throughout the Bible, names are important and offer insight and foreshadowing into the characters of those being named. By naming the sons Mahlon and Chilion, it seems that the author is trying to communicate something additional to the reader. According to Koehler-Baumgartner, Mahlon means "sickly person" (p. 569), and Chilion means "frailty" (p. 479). It will thus come as no surprise that they die early and unexpectedly. Moreover, the author wants to make sure that the reader knows that the new settlers in Moab came from a particular place in the Land of Israel.

Thus, he specifically identifies their city of origin. He uses the term *ephratim* as a term derived from a group or place (what linguists call a "gentilic"). Thus, Ephratites come from Ephrat. Then the author specifies that they came from Bethlehem in Judah.

The *Targum* explains *ephratim* as *rabbanim* (teachers, scholars) and adds that the men became part of *ruflin* (military tribunals). Perhaps the *Targum* wants to suggest that Elimelech and his family came to Moab as dignitaries, rather than as a refugee family fleeing the famine.

For Rashi, *ephratim* has two meanings: *chashuvim* (important people) and "people from Ephrat." Rashi finds proof in the Talmud that the men from Ephrat, now settled in Moab, were important people. He cites *Nazir* 23b, which posits that Eglon, king of Moab, gave his daughter Ruth in marriage to Mahlon.

Ibn Ezra chooses to interpret *ephratim* in two ways, but both differ from Rashi's choice of explanation. For Ibn Ezra, the word may refer either to the place (Ephrat) or to a family who is descended from the tribe of Ephraim. He also explains that—unlike Issachar and Moses—we do not know the reasons why Mahlon and Chilion received their names. Ibn Ezra also states that it is unlikely that the two brothers married the Moabite women until after they had converted to Judaism, although there is nothing in the text to indicate that his assumption is correct. It is probably more of a case of rabbinic apology for an oft-practiced custom in the ancient world of men marrying non-Jewish women. This embarrassed the commentators, and they felt compelled to respond to it.

אː‏ג וַיָּמָת אֱלִימֶלֶךְ אִישׁ נָעֳמִי וַתִּשָּׁאֵר הִיא וּשְׁנֵי בָנֶיהָ:

**1:3** ELIMELECH, NAOMI'S SPOUSE, DIED, AND SHE REMAINED
WITH HER TWO SONS.

The author seems to use the term *vatisha-eir* to make sure that the reader knows that Naomi remained in Moab instead of returning home. The *Targum* avoids such a conclusion, instead adding the word "widow" so that the verse reads that Naomi "remained a widow." A widow with young sons was in an extremely vulnerable position in ancient society. Similarly, the *Targum* adds the word "orphans" to amplify the plight of the two sons.

Rashi finds this verse to be the source of the rabbinic saying *Ein ish meit elah l'ishto*, "The impact of one's death is greatest upon a spouse" (Babylonian Talmud, *Sanhedrin* 22b). Moreover, Rashi explains that Elimelech dominated Naomi and made her secondary to him. As a result, he was affected by divine punishment, but she was not. Like all of us, Rashi searches for a reason when someone dies. He assigns responsibility to God but offers an acceptable reason for Elimelech's death, something that may have helped Rashi but does not resonate for the modern reader.

א:ד וַיִּשְׂאוּ לָהֶם נָשִׁים מֹאֲבִיּוֹת שֵׁם הָאַחַת עָרְפָּה וְשֵׁם הַשֵּׁנִית רוּת
וַיֵּשְׁבוּ שָׁם כְּעֶשֶׂר שָׁנִים:

**1:4** THE TWO MARRIED MOABITE WOMEN, ONE NAMED
ORPAH AND THE OTHER NAMED RUTH, AND LIVED
THERE ABOUT TEN YEARS.

The author subtly presents the reader with two intermarriages. One might expect a
discussion of the challenges implicit in intermarriage and the stress on family relations.
But the notion that the marriages lasted ten years testifies to the contrary. According to
the verses that follow, Naomi had a positive relationship with her daughters-in-law.
Thus, the author suggests that intermarriage, even with a woman from Moab, is not
inherently problematic.

Conversely, in the viewpoint of the *Targum*, intermarriage is a problem. As a result,
the *Targum* states explicitly that in marrying foreign women, particularly these two
from Moab, the two sons transgressed the ''decree of God.'' Despite the fact that the
*Targum* also notes that Ruth was the daughter of King Eglon and thus highborn, it
does not view these marriages in a positive light. The tension over intermarriage is
placed into the text by the commentators and does not seem to emerge organically
from it.

א:ה וַיָּמוּתוּ גַם־שְׁנֵיהֶם מַחְלוֹן וְכִלְיוֹן וַתִּשָּׁאֵר הָאִשָּׁה מִשְּׁנֵי יְלָדֶיהָ
וּמֵאִישָׁהּ:

**1:5** THE TWO OF THEM, MAHLON AND CHILION, ALSO
DIED. SO THE WOMAN WAS LEFT BEREFT OF HER TWO
CHILDREN AND HER SPOUSE.

In its commentary on verse 1:4, the *Targum* makes it clear why the two young
husbands die. Because of their transgressions, their days are cut short, and they die in
an unclean land. For the *Targum*, any place outside of Israel, particularly Moab, is
considered unclean, that is, not fit for the raising of a Jewish family.

Rashi finds importance in the phrase *gam sh'neihem* (also the two of them). He
understands it to mean that first the two brothers are punished by losing their money.
Then their camels die, followed by the rest of the herd. Finally, they themselves die.

To Ibn Ezra the word order of the last clause in the sentence, in which ''her
children'' is mentioned before ''her spouse,'' is an expression of Naomi's differ-
entiated pain. She mourns the loss of her two young sons more than her spouse, who
was already old. How can any commentator try to compare one loss over another!
Even if her spouse was old, it does not make his loss any less painful.

א:ו וַתָּקָם הִיא וְכַלֹּתֶיהָ וַתָּשָׁב מִשְּׂדֵי מוֹאָב כִּי שָׁמְעָה בִּשְׂדֵה מוֹאָב
כִּי־פָקַד יְהוָה אֶת־עַמּוֹ לָתֵת לָהֶם לָחֶם:

**1:6** SO SHE AROSE WITH HER TWO DAUGHTERS-IN-LAW
THAT SHE MIGHT RETURN FROM THE COUNTRY OF
MOAB, FOR IN THE COUNTRY OF MOAB SHE HAD
HEARD THAT *ADONAI* REMEMBERED THE PEOPLE,
GIVING THEM FOOD.

The first word of the verse, *vatakom* (literally, "and she arose"), suggests two idiomatic uses of the verb, both of which are valid in this context. It may suggest an action used by mourners following a death, as in Genesis 23:3, or it may anticipate an action. In this case, it anticipates Naomi's return to the Land of Israel once she rises from mourning.

However, Ibn Ezra explains that the problem with this verse is with the use of the verb *vatashov* (literally, "and she returned"), which we have translated as "that she might return." He argues that it is only in the next verse that we read that she has left Moab. Citing the parallel use of the verb in Joshua 24:9, he maintains that since Naomi intends to return, the Bible regards it as if she already has, hence the author's choice of verb tense.

It is not surprising that following such tragedy Naomi would want to return home, with all of its implications of nurture and support. Her action reflects the Hebrew idiom *M'shaneh makom, m'shaneh mazal*, "With a change of place comes a change of luck."

א:ז וַתֵּצֵא מִן־הַמָּקוֹם אֲשֶׁר הָיְתָה־שָׁמָּה וּשְׁתֵּי כַלֹּתֶיהָ עִמָּהּ וַתֵּלַכְנָה
בַדֶּרֶךְ לָשׁוּב אֶל־אֶרֶץ יְהוּדָה:

**1:7** TOGETHER WITH HER DAUGHTERS-IN-LAW, SHE LEFT
THE PLACE WHERE THEY HAD LIVED. AND THEY WENT
ON THE ROAD TO GO BACK TO THE LAND OF JUDAH.

Taking a perspective slightly different from the one Ibn Ezra took in the previous verse, Rashi raises the question: "Why does this verse use the verb *vateitzei* [and she left] if the previous verse contained the verb *vatashov* [and she returned]?" Had she not left she could not return. So Rashi tells his readers that the Bible is attempting to teach a lesson already taught in the story of Jacob (Genesis 28:10), that when a righteous person leaves a place, it makes an impression.

א:ח וַתֹּאמֶר נָעֳמִי לִשְׁתֵּי כַלֹּתֶיהָ לֵכְנָה שֹׁבְנָה אִשָּׁה לְבֵית אִמָּהּ יעשה
יַעַשׂ יְהֹוָה עִמָּכֶם חֶסֶד כַּאֲשֶׁר עֲשִׂיתֶם עִם־הַמֵּתִים וְעִמָּדִי:

**1:8** NOW NAOMI SAID TO HER TWO DAUGHTERS-IN-LAW,
"GO BACK, EACH OF YOU, TO YOUR MOTHER'S HOUSE.
MAY *ADONAI* DEAL AS KINDLY WITH YOU AS YOU HAVE
DEALT WITH THE DECEASED AND WITH ME.

Following the English idiom, we have translated *ishah l'veit imah* (literally, "each woman to her mother's house") as "each of you, to your mother's house." The *Targum* explains the "kindness" that the daughters-in-law afforded to their deceased husbands and to Naomi: although widowed, they refused to marry other men, and they supported their mother-in-law.

Ibn Ezra reminds the reader that "the deceased" (literally, "the dead") mentioned here are Naomi's sons.

This verse seems to reflect a dominant feminist theme. One might expect Naomi to suggest to her daughters-in-law that they return to their father's houses. But as the surviving matriarch, and as a literary parallel, she tells them to return to their mothers. Perhaps the bereft Naomi doesn't feel that she can offer them the support they need as grieving widows, since she is overwhelmed by her own grief. Nevertheless, she recognizes the kind of love that only their mothers will be able to offer.

א:ט יִתֵּן יְהֹוָה לָכֶם וּמְצֶאןָ מְנוּחָה אִשָּׁה בֵּית אִישָׁהּ וַתִּשַּׁק לָהֶן
וַתִּשֶּׂאנָה קוֹלָן וַתִּבְכֶּינָה:

**1:9** "MAY *ADONAI* GRANT THAT EACH OF YOU FIND
COMFORT IN THE HOUSE OF ANOTHER SPOUSE." THEN
SHE KISSED THEM, BUT THEY LIFTED THEIR VOICES
AND WEPT.

In the context of the ancient world, it makes sense that Naomi would want her daughters-in-law to remarry. A widow, especially one without children, was considered to be vulnerable and unprotected. The Torah often refers to the most defenseless in society as "the widowed and the orphaned" (Exodus 22:21–23; Deuteronomy 10:18). So Naomi asks God to provide a protecting spouse for them.

The *Targum* focuses on the word *yitein* (literally, "will give, grant") and translates the verse as "May *Adonai* give you a full reward for all the good that you have done for me, and may the reward be that each of you find comfort in another spouse's home." Ibn Ezra also focuses his comments on the word *yitein*. He understands the phrase simply and directly as "May *Adonai* give you a spouse." While we may assume that the *Targum* has relinquished its concern over the intermarriage, it is encouraging the daughters-in-law to stay in Moab—so that they aren't in a position to marry Israelite men again.

א:י וַתֹּאמַרְנָה־לָּהּ כִּי־אִתָּךְ נָשׁוּב לְעַמֵּךְ׃

**1:10** AND THEY SAID, "WE WANT TO GO BACK WITH YOU
TO YOUR PEOPLE."

Although "want" is not expressly stated, the content makes it clear that it is the sentiment the two women are trying to express. The *Targum* expands the text and adds to the response of the young women: "We will not return to our people and our religion. Rather, we want to return with you to your people to become converts to Judaism." This allows future commentators to build their case for Ruth's formal conversion to Judaism. It seems to us that what is of primary concern to those who join the Jewish people or marry into it is the desire to cast their lot among us, especially since formal acts of conversion were not required among ancient Jews.

א:יא וַתֹּאמֶר נָעֳמִי שֹׁבְנָה בְנֹתַי לָמָּה תֵלַכְנָה עִמִּי הַעוֹד־לִי בָנִים בְּמֵעַי
וְהָיוּ לָכֶם לַאֲנָשִׁים׃

**1:11** BUT NAOMI REFUSED. "MY DAUGHTERS, GO ON BACK.
WHAT IS THE POINT OF GOING WITH ME? DO I HAVE
ANY MORE SONS IN MY BELLY WHO COULD BE YOUR
SPOUSES?

As is demonstrated in Genesis 30:13, *bat*, usually translated as "daughter," can also mean "girl." *V'notai*, therefore, can either be translated as "my daughters" or "my girls." In both cases, it is a term of endearment. *Mei-ai*, which we have translated as "my belly," literally means "my bowels." It could mean "my body." The *Targum* translates the verse literally and makes Naomi's question to her daughters-in-law rather specific: "Do I have a fetus in my belly...?"

Ibn Ezra relates this verse to a controversy between the Rabbinites and Karaites concerning levirate marriage. He tells us that some Rabbinites thought that this verse provided proof for the requirement of levirate marriage from a source other than the Torah. However, unless there was some flexibility in the practice during the ancient period—for which we have no evidence—it seems that he does not realize that the practice applied to the brothers of the deceased husband and not the brothers of the widow. There might have been different legal interpretations among the Rabbis before the law was codified, but biblical law was clear. While her voice seems filled with pathos, Naomi is simply speaking poetically. She has no other children. Had she other sons, she would allow them to marry her daughters-in-law, so that they might fulfill the legal requirement of marrying the surviving sibling.

אִיב שֹׁבְנָה בְנֹתַי לֵכְןָ כִּי זָקַנְתִּי מִהְיוֹת לְאִישׁ כִּי אָמַרְתִּי יֶשׁ־לִי תִקְוָה
גַּם הָיִיתִי הַלַּיְלָה לְאִישׁ וְגַם יָלַדְתִּי בָנִים:

**1:12** "DAUGHTERS, GO ON BACK. I AM TOO OLD TO GET MARRIED. EVEN IF I THOUGHT THAT I HAD ANY HOPE, EVEN IF I WERE WITH A MAN TONIGHT, EVEN IF I WERE TO BEAR SONS…

Naomi just wants to be left alone in her grief. Perhaps the lingering presence of her daughters-in-law reminds her of the death of her two sons—a pain understandably too great for her to bear.

The *Targum* expands its translation of the verse to tell the two young women to go back to their own people. By focusing on the words *ki zakanti* (I am old), the *Targum* explains why Naomi is without hope. If she were younger, she would be optimistic about the prospect of marrying again and having more children. She feels that she is too old to start again, but her daughters-in-law are young enough to do so.

Rashi's comment emphasizes the struggle of the commentators over the acceptance of the interfaith marriages of Naomi's sons. In order to resolve what appears to be a contradiction of biblical law, Rashi suggests that were Naomi able to marry and bear sons, they could be married to the young women without any concern about either the prohibition of engaging in sexual relations with the wife of one's brother (Leviticus 20:21) or the requirement of levirate marriage (Deuteronomy 25:5–6), because when the two young women were married to Mahlon and Chilion, her deceased sons, they were neither Jewish nor converts to Judaism. Thus, they would not be breaking the law, since it applied only to Jews. Now that they have offered to be converted, marriage with her theoretical new sons would have been permitted. Rashi explains that the phrase beginning *ki amarti* (literally, "I said," translated here as "if I thought") means "if my heart said to me to marry again and bear children, even were I to conceive males tonight, and even were I to bear sons," which leads to the conclusion of this thought in the next verse.

אַ:יג הֲלָהֵן תְּשַׂבֵּרְנָה עַד אֲשֶׁר יִגְדָּלוּ הֲלָהֵן תֵּעָגֵנָה לְבִלְתִּי הֱיוֹת לְאִישׁ אַל בְּנֹתַי כִּי־מַר־לִי מְאֹד מִכֶּם כִּי־יָצְאָה בִי יַד־יְהֹוָה:

**1:13** "WOULD YOU WAIT FOR THEM UNTIL THEY WERE GROWN? WOULD YOU KEEP YOURSELVES FROM MARRIAGE BECAUSE OF THEM? OH MY DAUGHTERS, DON'T DO IT! I AM EVEN WORSE OFF THAN YOU ARE, BECAUSE *ADONAI'S* HAND HAS MOVED AGAINST ME."

The word *tei-ageinah* occurs only here in the *Tanach*. We have translated it as "keep yourself from marriage." It is the source of the word *agunah* (literally, "a chained woman," who is prevented from remarrying). In translating this, the *Targum* uses a similar word (with the root *a-g-m*, instead of *a-g-n*) to mean "you will be prevented from marriage" (literally, "sitting bent") and adds "like a woman waiting for a young boy to grow into adulthood." The *Targum* also expands Naomi's plea to her daughters-in-law: "Please don't [further] embitter my soul, because I feel more bitter than you."

Deriving his explanation from the Mishnaic phrase *ag ugah* (he drew a circle [*Mishnah Taanit* 3:8]), Rashi explains that the word *tei-ageinah* means "bound."

Rashi and Ibn Ezra differ as to the meaning of the phrase "God's hand." For Rashi, it is an indication of murrain, a cattle disease, as in Exodus 9:3. For Ibn Ezra, it is the way humans explain that God's decree has been leveled against a person.

Each phrase reveals more of Naomi's grief. Yet, in what seems to be an expression of altruism, she encourages her daughters-in-law to "get on with their lives." Were Naomi even in a position to get married and have children, it would be unrealistic for the women to wait until these theoretical sons grew old enough to procreate with them.

אַ:יד וַתִּשֶּׂנָה קוֹלָן וַתִּבְכֶּינָה עוֹד וַתִּשַּׁק עָרְפָּה לַחֲמוֹתָהּ וְרוּת דָּבְקָה בָּהּ:

**1:14** THEY AGAIN BURST OUT CRYING. ORPAH KISSED HER MOTHER-IN-LAW GOODBYE, BUT RUTH CLUNG TO HER.

The sense here is that these young women love their mother-in-law and don't want to leave her. They have also grown close to the people of Israel and do not want to separate themselves out.

The *Targum* expands the translation of "again" and adds the words *zimnah ochranah* (one further time).

א:טו וַתֹּאמֶר הִנֵּה שָׁבָה יְבִמְתֵּךְ אֶל־עַמָּהּ וְאֶל־אֱלֹהֶיהָ שׁוּבִי אַחֲרֵי
יְבִמְתֵּךְ:

**1:15** NAOMI SAID TO HER, "YOUR SISTER-IN-LAW HAS GONE
BACK TO HER PEOPLE AND HER GODS. GO, DO WHAT
YOUR SISTER-IN-LAW HAS DONE."

Naomi assumes that her daughters-in-law were drawn to Judaism as a result of their
relationship with her sons. Thus, her advice is not surprising. What is more surprising
is that while Orpah heeds Naomi's advice, Ruth does not. Ruth appears to be a
stronger, more independent woman than her sister-in-law.

For the *Targum*, there cannot be the possibility of other gods, so it translates "her
gods" as "that which she fears" and adds *l'amaych v'ldachaltach* (to your people and
that which you fear) to Naomi's statement to Ruth. This is similar to the tendency of
contemporary prayer books to translate *elohim* in the first line of the *Mi Chamochah*
as "mighty" rather than "gods."

Rashi takes note that the accent on the word *shavah* is on the first syllable. He
explains that the word is thus in the past tense, meaning "she has gone back." Had
the accent been on the second syllable, it could have been read as "she goes back."

Ibn Ezra points out that the uncommon word *y'vimteich* follows the use in the
Torah of *y'vimto* (brother's widow [Deuteronomy 25:7, 25:9]). Its sense as "sister-in-
law" occurs only here. He also takes the phrase "gone back to her gods" as an
indication that Orpah converted to Judaism in the past and now is about to revert to
her original beliefs, the implication being that her conversion was not sincere. Had
Naomi been more welcoming, and had Ibn Ezra interpreted the verse more
generously, perhaps the pervasive negative attitudes toward Jews-by-choice could
have been changed earlier in the history of the Jewish people. These unwelcoming
attitudes continue to be seen in some sectors of the Jewish community even today.

א:טז וַתֹּאמֶר רוּת אַל־תִּפְגְּעִי־בִי לְעָזְבֵךְ לָשׁוּב מֵאַחֲרָיִךְ כִּי אֶל־אֲשֶׁר
תֵּלְכִי אֵלֵךְ וּבַאֲשֶׁר תָּלִינִי אָלִין עַמֵּךְ עַמִּי וֵאלֹהַיִךְ אֱלֹהָי:

**1:16** BUT RUTH SAID, "DON'T BEG ME TO LEAVE YOU OR
TO KEEP FROM FOLLOWING YOU, BECAUSE WHEREVER
YOU GO, I WILL GO. WHEREVER YOU STAY, I WILL STAY.
YOUR PEOPLE WILL BE MY PEOPLE. AND YOUR GOD
WILL BE MY GOD.

This is Ruth's most famous statement, which has become the signature statement of
Jews-by-choice. It is beautiful poetry without the need for explanation or further
explication. For the commentators though, it is insufficient. They want to use the

opportunity to teach converts to Judaism their responsibilities. At the same time, they remind the born-Jewish reader of basic tenets of Judaism as well. While the approach may seem a bit off-putting, it is likely that they are trying to avoid a double standard, a posture that contemporary Jews would do well to emulate.

The *Targum* adds the words "for I wish to be converted" after the words "from following you" in Ruth's statement. It also provides the terms of conversion in an expanded exchange between Naomi and Ruth. Naomi says, "We are commanded that in observing the Sabbath and holy days, we are not permitted to walk more than 2,000 cubits." Ruth responds, "Wherever you walk, I will walk." Naomi continues, "We are directed not to spend the night alone with the nations [that is, with a non-Jew]," and Ruth replies, "However you stay [spend the night], I will stay [spend the night]." Naomi says further, "We are instructed to keep 613 *mitzvot.*" Ruth says, "Whatever your people keeps, I will keep, as if they were my people before this." And Naomi says, "We are forbidden idol worship." Ruth then concludes, "Your God will be my God."

Rashi translates the word *tifg'i* as "urge." From among its many possible meanings, we have translated it as "beg." Rashi then notes that the Rabbis (Babylonian Talmud, *Y'vamot* 47b) deduced from this verse that when people want to convert to Judaism, we are obligated to warn them of some of the punishments that result from transgressions so that if they then want to change their minds, they can still do so. Rashi also reads the second part of Ruth's response, "However you spend the night, I will spend the night," as a reply to Naomi telling her, "A woman is forbidden to be alone at night with a man other than her husband."

Ibn Ezra takes the words "your people" to indicate a commitment on Ruth's part to the Torah and the God of Israel.

בַּאֲשֶׁר תָּמוּתִי אָמוּת וְשָׁם אֶקָּבֵר כֹּה יַעֲשֶׂה יְהֹוָה לִי וְכֹה יֹסִיף כִּי א:יז
הַמָּוֶת יַפְרִיד בֵּינִי וּבֵינֵךְ:

1:17 "WHERE YOU DIE, THERE WILL I DIE AND THERE WILL I BE BURIED. MAY *ADONAI* DO WHATEVER [*ADONAI*] WILL TO ME IF ANYTHING BUT DEATH SEPARATES YOU FROM ME."

Ruth continues her passionate statement and plea to Naomi. By employing the dramatic image of death, an experience unfortunately fresh for both Naomi and Ruth, she reminds us that ultimately little else matters beyond being together.

The words *ko yaaseh Adonai li v'choh yosif* (literally, "thus may *Adonai* do to me and thus may [*Adonai*] increase") call upon God to act as a guarantor of any action by invoking a curse directed by the speaker against a person who fails to comply. In this case, Ruth is invoking the curse against herself should she not fulfill the promise of her oath. The formula is more often found with the word *Elohim* rather than *Adonai*. (See I Samuel 3:17, 14:44, II Kings 6:31. The formula appears without the words *lo yosif* in I Samuel 27:11. In I Kings 19:2 and 20:10, the word *elohim* appears to be used to refer to pagan gods.)

Because of the way the *Targum* translates ''where you die,'' questions about the dating of the *Targum* and Mishnah can be raised, as is noted in the introduction to this volume (see p. xv). The *Targum* takes the words *v'choh yosif* as if Ruth said to Naomi, *v'lo tosifi*, ''Don't continue'' to speak to me, and then adds the words to the formula for the curse.

Rashi's comments follow the reading of the *Targum*. He reads this verse as Naomi warning Ruth about the four methods of execution. However, he adds that the phrase ''there will I be buried'' suggests that Naomi warned Ruth that there were two separate cemeteries for those executed: one for those who were stoned and burnt, the other for those beheaded and strangled. The Sages suggested that the type of execution, and thus burial, depended on the severity of the transgression (Babylonian Talmud, *Sanhedrin* 47b). Ancient burials involved a two-stage process. Persons were buried, and then after a period of time, the remains were dug up and reburied. Apparently, the Sages did not want to mix the bones of the righteous with bones of the sinners. What is significant here is not so much the details of the Rabbis' debate over execution and burial, but rather that Rashi's reading identifies Naomi as Ruth's teacher, educating her about Judaism. Rashi goes on to turn the formula for making a curse into a statement by Ruth. Although God treated her badly by taking her husband and impoverishing her, the only thing worse that God could do would be to have death separate her from Naomi, something that God has refrained from doing.

אוֹיח וַתֵּרֶא כִּי־מִתְאַמֶּצֶת הִיא לָלֶכֶת אִתָּהּ וַתֶּחְדַּל לְדַבֵּר אֵלֶיהָ׃

**1:18** WHEN NAOMI SAW HOW INTENT SHE [RUTH] WAS TO GO WITH HER, SHE STOPPED ARGUING WITH HER.

Rashi says that this verse is derived from a rabbinic statement (Babylonian Talmud, *Y'vamot* 47b) that teaches that one should not add more restrictions to potential converts to Judaism, but rather they should be welcomed once the depth of their conviction is made clear.

א:יט וַתֵּלַכְנָה שְׁתֵּיהֶם עַד־בֹּאָנָה בֵּית לָחֶם וַיְהִי כְּבֹאָנָה בֵּית לֶחֶם
וַתֵּהֹם כָּל־הָעִיר עֲלֵיהֶן וַתֹּאמַרְנָה הֲזֹאת נָעֳמִי:

**1:19** SO THE TWO WENT ON UNTIL THEY REACHED
BETHLEHEM. WHEN THEY ARRIVED THERE, THE ENTIRE
CITY CHATTERED ABOUT THEM. SOME WOMEN ASKED,
"IS IT REALLY NAOMI?"

People seem to always talk about newcomers, as well as gossiping about people who move away and return to their community, especially when there are many changes in their lives. On one level, this verse seems like a reflection of normative group behavior.

The word *vateihom* is onomatopoeic. While it comes from the root *hamam*, it is difficult to translate. According to Koehler-Baumgartner (p. 251), the simple active form of the verb means "to bring motion and confusion." The simple passive form means "to be beside oneself." The sense here seems to be "to hum with conversation" or, as we have translated it, that their arrival caused a great chattering.

The *Targum* translates *vateihom* as *v'argishu* (stirred up, troubled). Thus, it translates part of the verse as "all the dwellers in the city were stirred, troubled because of them."

Rashi quotes the statement of Rabbi Abahu found in the midrash *Ruth Rabbah* 3:5 (in some editions it is Rabbi Y'hudah bar Simon instead) that Jews-by-choice are so precious in God's eyes that as soon as Ruth declared her intention to convert to Judaism, the Bible equated her with Naomi. That's why the verse says, "so the two went." He takes *vateihom* to indicate that the commotion of the entire city was because people were on their way to bury Boaz's wife who had died that day, rather than due to the arrival of Naomi and Ruth. According to Rashi, some women ask, "Is it really Naomi?" because they were used to seeing her travel in carriages rather than on foot, an indication of how far down she had come in the world.

Ibn Ezra points out that *vateihom* is a simple passive form from the root *hamam* and, like Rashi, explains the women's question as a sign of Naomi's changed circumstances. Elimelech and Naomi had been wealthy people. Now Naomi returns like a pauper.

א:כ וַתֹּאמֶר אֲלֵיהֶן אַל־תִּקְרֶאנָה לִי נָעֳמִי קְרֶאןָ לִי מָרָא כִּי־הֵמַר שַׁדַּי לִי מְאֹד:

**1:20** SHE ANSWERED THEM, "DON'T CALL ME NAOMI [PLEASANTNESS], CALL ME MARAH [BITTERNESS], FOR THE ALMIGHTY HAS MADE MY LIFE EXCEPTIONALLY BITTER.

Naomi's words serve to tell people that she is not the same person she was when they last saw her. Life has changed her greatly. The *Targum* expands Naomi's statement to read, "call me Marah [bitter] of soul." Ibn Ezra explains that the name Naomi is derived from *noam*, meaning "sweetness" and hence, "pleasure." He explains Marah, derived from *mar*, as its reverse, meaning "bitterness" and hence, "pain."

א:כא אֲנִי מְלֵאָה הָלַכְתִּי וְרֵיקָם הֱשִׁיבַנִי יְהוָה לָמָּה תִקְרֶאנָה לִי נָעֳמִי וַיהוָה עָנָה בִי וְשַׁדַּי הֵרַע לִי:

**1:21** "I LEFT HERE FULL. *ADONAI* HAS BROUGHT ME BACK EMPTY. WHY CALL ME NAOMI? *ADONAI* HAS TESTIFIED AGAINST ME. THE ALMIGHTY HAS TREATED ME BADLY."

Naomi's bitterness spills out in every word of this verse. While she knows not why, she believes that God is intentionally punishing her—a normal, human reaction, especially for a religious woman.

The verb *anah* presents us with a challenge in translating. As Koehler-Baumgartner points out (pp. 852–853), the verb in its simple form (which Hebrew linguists refer to as the *kal* form) means "answer, reply" or "testify" in legal contexts. A homonym for *anah* in the same form means "to be wretched" or "to cringe." In the more intensive form (the *pi-eil* form), the verb means "to oppress, humiliate, do violence." The context of the last clause, containing the verb *heira* (has treated me badly), suggests that *anah* should provide a parallel. As a result, *anah* would be translated as "oppressed [me]." However, the verb appears in the text in the simple rather than the intensive form. Since the meanings of the homonym do not seem to fit, we have followed the *Targum* and translated *anah* as "has testified."

The *Targum* embellishes the word "full" by adding "with my husband and sons" and explains "testified" as "testified as my transgression." The *Targum* is also careful to avoid any anthropomorphism, translating "*Adonai*" as "from before *Adonai*."

Rashi offers two explanations of "full": "[filled] with wealth and children" and "she was pregnant." He also gives two explanations for "testified": "*Adonai* testified to an awareness of my wickedness" or that she was affected by the divine quality of justice. Ibn Ezra explains "full" in the same manner as does Rashi. He also gives two explanations of *anah*: to humble oneself or to act as witness. Rashi prefers the second meaning rather than the first. Furthermore, he explains "treated me badly" as "smitten [me]" or "treated me badly because of my sins." Rashi is helping Naomi to discern a reason for her state of being. Thus, he thinks his last explanation is the most appropriate.

א:כב וַתָּשָׁב נָעֳמִי וְרוּת הַמּוֹאֲבִיָּה כַלָּתָהּ עִמָּהּ הַשָּׁבָה מִשְּׂדֵי מוֹאָב וְהֵמָּה בָּאוּ בֵּית לֶחֶם בִּתְחִלַּת קְצִיר שְׂעֹרִים:

**1:22** SO NAOMI RETURNED WITH HER DAUGHTER-IN-LAW, RUTH THE MOABITE, FROM THE LAND OF MOAB. THEY ARRIVED IN BETHLEHEM AT THE TIME OF THE BARLEY HARVEST.

The chapter concludes with Naomi coming home. The author is trying to express her homecoming as a note of hope, alluded to in the motif of the harvest, and a change from her recent experiences.

The word order of the Hebrew appears to be redundant. The verse literally reads, "So Naomi returned and Ruth, the Moabite, with her returned from the country of Moab," using two different Hebrew words for "returned." This may be due to the author's desire to stress the fact that Ruth willingly left Moab, the country of her people. Moreover, the author wants to emphasize the feeling of return that accompanies those who come to the Land of Israel.

The *Targum* expands "the time of the barley harvest" to "the eve of the Day of Passover, the day when the Israelites begin harvesting the omer of the heave offering of barley." Again, Passover offers the reader hope and a sense of renewal. It is also possible that the *Targum* wants to connect Ruth to Shavuot through this passage.

Whereas Rashi simply follows the *Targum*, Ibn Ezra sees the repetition of "she returned" as a way of linking the return of Naomi and Ruth to the harvest of barley, which comes to play a significant role in the story.

## Moab

Moab is a country neighboring ancient Israel that lies to the east of the Jordan River and the Dead Sea, which, along with the country of Ammon, made up what is the contemporary kingdom of Jordan. The origins of these two countries can be traced back in the Torah to the incestuous union of Lot, Abraham's nephew, and his two daughters (Genesis 19:30–38). Often Moab and Ammon are discussed together as if they are two parts of the same country. The Bible recognizes a close but contentious relationship between these two nations and the Israelite nation. They share much in common with one another. For example, like Hebrew, the Moabite language is a dialect of the Canaanite. As a result, they were mutually intelligible. Throughout its history (independent beginning ca. thirteenth/twelfth century B.C.E.), Moab was often at odds with various tribes of Israel. Soon after David became king of Israel, he conquered Moab and incorporated it into Israel. Sometime later, probably after the death of Solomon, Moab declared its independence (ca. 922 B.C.E.), only to be subjugated by a later Israelite king, Omri (ca. 880 B.C.E.). A few decades later, Moab became independent once again (mid-ninth century B.C.E.).

It is perhaps because of this ongoing tension that the Book of Deuteronomy includes a declaration that Moabites cannot enter the Jewish community (Deuteronomy 23:4). This was interpreted to mean that an Israelite woman could not marry a man from Moab. However, the reverse seemed not to be the case, since Ruth married an Israelite. Later, the Talmud (*Y'vamot* 77a) explicitly relaxed its attitude toward those from Moab, claiming that the original Moabites could no longer be distinguished from other people.

# The Babylonian Exile

The Babylonian exile dates from 586 to 538 B.C.E. Some scholars mark the beginning as 597 B.C.E., when large numbers of the inhabitants of Judah were deported to Babylonia, rather than the year in which the Babylonian king Nebuchadnezzar destroyed the Temple in Jerusalem. The traditional notion of exile is that God punished the Jewish people, destroyed the Temple, and dispersed them throughout the world as punishment for not fulfilling their part of the covenant. Referred to as *galut* (or *galus*), it represents not only a physical state but also a longing to return to the Land of Israel.

# Karaites

The Karaites may be literally referred to as "scripturalists." The adherents of this religious group, which can be traced to Babylonia in the eighth century C.E., developed a system of law independent of the Talmud based on a literal interpretation of Scripture. The Karaites claim that their form of Judaism predates the rabbinic or Rabbinite model, which accepts the authority of the "Oral Law," the Mishnah and Talmud. As a result, their practices differ from Judaism, which is informed by the rabbinic teachings recorded in the Oral Law. For example, the Karaite calendar is based on the phases of the moon. Thus, holidays (except for Shavuot, which is always on Sunday) can occur on any day of the week. Biblical holidays are observed for only one day, and Chanukah, which does not appear in the Bible, is not celebrated at all. When Karaites pray, they remove their shoes. They kneel during prayer, and their synagogues are without chairs. *T'fillin* are not worn for prayer.

Strong Karaite communities flourished during the Middle Ages. While there was at times tremendous hostility toward them on the part of the rabbinic authorities, they never posed a significant threat to rabbinic communities. While small communities of Karaites remain in places like Turkey, France, and even San Francisco, the largest communities today are in Ashdod and Ramla in Israel.

## Rabbinites

The word "Rabbinites" was originally a derogatory term used by the Karaites to refer to those who followed rabbinic tradition. However, it is now primarily a technical term to refer to those who laid the foundation of Judaism as we know it.

## Levirate Marriage

Biblical law (Deuteronomy 25:5–6) requires that the brother of a man who died childless marry his brother's widow so that she may bear children in his brother's name. If the surviving brother does not want to marry his deceased brother's widow, then the ceremony of *chalitzah*, as described in Deuteronomy 25:7–10, must be performed. The ceremony is to be performed in front of five rabbinic judges. The passage from Deuteronomy is read by the widow. She removes a shoe, specially made for this purpose, from the surviving brother. Then she spits on the ground in front of him. This is a symbolic sign of rebuke and contempt for his shirking of responsibility. The chief rabbi of Israel issued a ruling in 1950 that eliminated the requirement of levirate marriage, but it remains an issue in the ultra-Orthodox *chareidi* communities.

## Agunah

The root related to the term *agunah* first occurs in the Book of Ruth (1:13). It refers to the status of a woman who is legally prohibited from marriage either because there is insufficient evidence that her husband has died or because he has been unwilling to give her a *get*, a Jewish divorce document. This is particularly problematic for women whose spouses are missing in action during wartime. The Talmud does allow for provisions to alleviate the burden somewhat, including, for example, the testimony of witnesses who, in other cases, would not be acceptable. Nevertheless, this legal conundrum presents a challenge for many traditional Jewish women, particularly when their spouses abandon them and refuse to grant them a divorce or withhold the granting of a *get* as a way to achieve financial or custody concessions. Although the Reform Movement accepts a civil divorce as sufficient for remarriage, the Conservative and Orthodox Movements require a *get*. Some Orthodox authorities, as well as the entire Conservative rabbinate, require a prenuptial agreement that commits the husband to appear before a rabbinical court should it be necessary and allows for the community to force his hand. The Reform Movement has rejected the notion of an *agunah* entirely because of issues of equality between women and men.

## Omer

An omer is a measure of barley. While the counting of the Omer, which takes place in the evening worship service from the second night of Passover until Shavuot, begins as a countdown to the barley harvest, culminating in the festival of Shavuot, it has taken on a spiritual dimension, particularly because of mystical influences in Judaism. The Omer period is represented by a matrix of the attributes of God that color each day of counting. As we count, we try to commune with God and luxuriate in the particular confluence of attributes designated for that particular day.

# GLEANINGS

## Intermarriage

As more people intermarry, intermarriage itself obviously becomes less an expression of deviance (in the sense of a desire to flee from one's own community) and more a function of opportunity. A structuralist approach would predict that greater acceptance of Jews by non-Jews, plus wider exposure to people from other backgrounds and greater mixing with them at school, in the workplace, and socially, make intermarriage more common. This view is consistent with data that show that those who intermarry are likely to be older at the time of marriage than their peers who married within their faith, and hence to have had more time to meet more diverse people.

Susan Weidman Schneider, Intermarriage: The Challenge of Living with Differences Between Christians and Jews (New York: The Free Press, 1989), 17

## Conversion Is a Process

Conversion to Judaism is a process, not a product. It's great that many Jewish leaders now are responding to the reality of interfaith marriage with a determination to reach out to Jews with gentile partners. But it makes me uneasy to hear the task defined as: "We have to convert them." That's too mechanical.

Of course, as a Jew by Choice, I am delighted to feel that the community now sees me and others like me as desirable. But I also know that conversion is part of a long, individual journey. We need to provide more guides along the path, not timekeepers at the end of the course, clocking numbers crossing the finish line.

Rachel Cowan, *Moment* 16, no. 2 (April 1991): 11

## *Embracing the Journey*

Just as a river may flow and flow and eventually reach the sea, so, too, may a searching soul eventually find a home. To a Jew-by-Choice, the path to Judaism may have begun long ago and in a far-distant place. The course of the journey may have been rocky and difficult, winding and obscure. For some, it meant leaving family and friends, finding new paths and making new trails. For others, it was a gentle continuation of something they glimpsed from afar in their childhood, something which seemed vaguely familiar and warm. For still others, the passage was storm-tossed and tumultuous, causing wrenching changes in their lives and in the lives of others around them. For all, the journey was life-transforming....And though the destination of each convert may be the same, each travels a path which is highly personal.

For just as it is written that there are 600,000 letters in the Torah—one for each Jewish soul which came out of bondage in Egypt—so, too, each soul has a different story and approaches God in his or her own way, a way that speaks to that soul as could no other path or journey.

Allan L. Berkowitz and Patti Moskowitz, eds. *Embracing the Covenant:*<br>*Converts to Judaism Talk About Why and How*<br>(Woodstock, VT: Jewish Lights Publishing, 1998), 53–54

## *Welcoming People to the Family*

We are a family, a growing family, which an increasing number of Americans not born or raised as Jews seek to join. This old-new rite of passage welcomes Jews-by-choice who seek to identify themselves with our community of faith. Given the increasing interest of spiritual seekers to become Jews-by-choice, conversion has taken on a life-cycle of its own. Through the act of conversion, the new Jew-by-choice becomes like one reborn, ready to be warmly welcomed and nurtured by the newly chosen community. Yet, there are voices who oppose opening the gates to non-Jewish spiritual seekers. They reflect the myth that proactive conversion that encourages non-Jews to become Jewish is contrary to the principles and practices of Judaism. The myth has cast a large shadow over the mitzvah of conversion....

Jews-by-choice are to be viewed not as surrogates for our lagging birth rates or as making up for our Holocaust losses. They are to be seen as serious men and women who have searched their hearts and minds and chosen to attach themselves to our family. They contribute to the enhancement of our spiritual life and in turn are deepened through the wisdom and values of the tradition of our family.

Harold M. Schulweis, *Finding Each Other in Judaism:*
*Meditations on the Rites of Passage from Birth to Immortality*
(New York: UAHC Press, 2001), 66–67

## Why I Am a Jew

In the twilight of the twentieth century, with people trying on varying parts of and even *whole* religions like shoppers trying on clothing in a bargain basement, anyone who remains a Jew must be considered a "Jew by choice." Unfortunately, choosing one's way over another's risks chauvinism.

Chauvinism is a distorted love of self achieved through denigrating others just as self-hate is a distorted love of others achieved through denigrating oneself. They are both variations of the same primary insecurity. Being a Jew may be the right choice and, indeed, the only viable one for most Jews. But not because Judaism is better (or worse) than any other religion. . . .

Imagine a deck of fifty-two religious playing cards. Each one represents a different, primary religious idea, such as salvation, love of neighbor, God, afterlife, guilt, charity, revelation, and the like. Any decent religion must—in order to be a religion—play with a full deck. The difference between one religion and another is the "order of the cards," the "stack of the deck." In one spiritual tradition, the first card is "salvation," while "revelation" doesn't show up until card number forty-three. In another religion, the order may be reversed. What, we must ask ourselves, would be the top cards in the Jewish deck?

Lawrence Kushner, *Eyes Remade for Wonder: A Lawrence Kushner Reader*
(Woodstock, VT: Jewish Lights Publishing, 1998), 213

## A Cosmology of Mourning

When the man I loved died, I read [Stephen] Levine and [Elisabeth] Kübler-Ross and gratefully accepted their adjurations not to stifle my grief, to welcome and feel fully each of its inevitable stages. I wept every day for two years. This new psychological perspective on grief probably saved my life, and I am thankful that a "stiff upper lip" is no longer considered a virtue. But for all my willingness to face and express feelings, something was missing for me at the time of my grieving. I needed a deeper understanding of death and of my own heartbreak.

Grief is not only a psychological response to a mystery. It is part of the mystery itself. Mourning is an essential process of *tikkun* (repair) by which the world can continue to function. Jewish tradition is rich in ritual which helps people survive the death of a loved one. And this ritual is grounded in a particular cosmology, without which the ritual may be comforting, but does not make philosophical sense. . . .

There is no teacher like mourning. Now that death has come close to me, both by taking the man I once loved and then by almost taking me, I am not the person I was before. I can only describe the change in the most personal terms. I am so glad to be alive, so grateful that my parents are alive and healthy, so thankful that I went on to love another man and make such an interesting and enjoyable life with him. I am richly blessed to live in a loving community in a beautiful place.

Yet, it could all go in a minute. It *will* all go in a minute. This life is a brief stop, whether I die tomorrow or in fifty years. I would love not to know this, to have the innocent certainty that, when loved ones set out on a journey, they will return unharmed, that I can go out to sea in my boat, play in the waves and not be swallowed up. But I am more grateful now than I ever was in my innocence.

In the end it is all a gift, is it not? The brief entwinement of body and soul, the breath of God that gives and sustains human life, creates such a colorful, sparkling trail as it arcs though time. It is so ephemeral, and yet it affects everything. As we say when we open our eyes every morning, ''I give thanks to You, God of life who is eternal, for returning my soul to me this morning. Great is Your faithfulness.''

Margaret Holub, ''A Cosmology of Mourning,'' in *Lifecycles:*
*Jewish Women on Life Passages and Personal Milestones*, vol. 1, ed. Debra Orenstein
(Woodstock, VT: Jewish Lights Publishing, 1994), 341, 350–351

# CHAPTER TWO

ב:א וּלְנָעֳמִי מידע מוֹדַע לְאִישָׁהּ אִישׁ גִּבּוֹר חַיִל מִמִּשְׁפַּחַת אֱלִימֶלֶךְ
וּשְׁמוֹ בֹּעַז:

**2:1** Now Naomi had an acquaintance belonging to
the family of Elimelech, her husband, an important person named Boaz.

Naomi is now back in Israel and has to start the process of putting her life back
together. Boaz, the person who will figure prominently in Naomi's spiritual and
financial rehabilitation, is introduced through his lineage.

The phrase *gibor chayil* can mean a "man of valor," or "brave man," as in Judges
11:1. In the plural form, *giborei chayalim* can mean "soldiers," as in I Chronicles 7:5.
In this context, we believe that "an important person" is an appropriate modern
translation. The *Targum* takes the words to mean "a powerful person, strong in
Torah."

The word *moda* (acquaintance) is read by Rashi to mean "relative." He deduces
from the Talmud (*Bava Batra* 91a) that Boaz was Elimelech's nephew: Elimelech,
Salmon (the father of Boaz), and Ploni Almoni (whom we will meet in chapter 4) were
the sons of the renowned Nahshon ben Aminadav (see Numbers 1:7, 2:3, 7:12, 7:17,
10:14). Rashi notes that even the merit of such a father was insufficient to protect
Elimelech, since he left the Land and settled outside of it.

On the basis of its use in Proverbs 7:4, Ibn Ezra also understands *moda* as
"relative." He follows the identification in the Talmud (*Bava Batra* 91a) of Boaz as the
judge Ibzan (Judges 12:8, 12:10), in keeping with the idea from the verse that he is
someone important.

ב:ב וַתֹּאמֶר רוּת הַמּוֹאֲבִיָּה אֶל־נָעֳמִי אֵלְכָה־נָּא הַשָּׂדֶה וַאֲלַקֳטָה
בַשִּׁבֳּלִים אַחַר אֲשֶׁר אֶמְצָא־חֵן בְּעֵינָיו וַתֹּאמֶר לָהּ לְכִי בִתִּי:

2:2 RUTH, THE MOABITE WOMAN, SAID TO NAOMI,
"I WOULD LIKE TO GO INTO THE FIELD SO I CAN
GLEAN EARS OF GRAIN, FOLLOWING AFTER SOME MAN
IN WHOSE EYES I MIGHT FIND FAVOR." NAOMI REPLIED,
"GO, MY DAUGHTER."

This verse reflects the reality of the period in which the story of Ruth takes place. Historically, women needed protection. Bereft of her husband, Ruth seeks to find another. Understanding her need, Naomi encourages Ruth, even though Ruth's behavior is quite bold. This verse also assumes familiarity with the mitzvah of *leket*, "gleanings" (Leviticus 23:22), which allows the poor and the stranger to pick up what the harvesters have left behind at harvest time. Both meanings of the word *achar* (either "after" in space or "later" in time) fit the context. The context suggests a reference to a male: "after some man" or "later than some man," rather than "after someone" or "later than someone," since those who reaped the field were men.

The *Targum* translates *chein* (favor) as *rachamim* (compassion). Rashi understands Ruth's statement as "Let me go to one of the fields of the men of the city, and the one in whose eyes I will find favor will not berate me [for gleaning]."

Ibn Ezra presents the reader with two possible identifications for "the one in whose eyes I might find favor." That person may be Boaz, or he may be the unnamed owner of the field.

ב:ג וַתֵּלֶךְ וַתָּבוֹא וַתְּלַקֵּט בַּשָּׂדֶה אַחֲרֵי הַקֹּצְרִים וַיִּקֶר מִקְרֶהָ חֶלְקַת
הַשָּׂדֶה לְבֹעַז אֲשֶׁר מִמִּשְׁפַּחַת אֱלִימֶלֶךְ:

2:3 SO SHE WENT AND CAME TO A FIELD, WHERE SHE
GLEANED AFTER THE REAPERS. NOW JUST BY CHANCE,
IT HAPPENED THAT THE FIELD WAS OWNED BY BOAZ OF
THE FAMILY OF ELIMELECH.

Some may read this verse as a chance encounter. Others may read this as a meeting orchestrated by God. It is possible that the author is employing irony in the use of "just by chance," as a way to direct the reader's attention to Ruth's provocative behavior. There is a practical side to it, too. Without any economic support, Ruth must seek food for herself and Naomi. Rashi quotes a midrash (*Ruth Rabbah* 4:6) in which the author suggests that the words "she went and came" indicate that Ruth had marked out the particular field and left markers on the way there to make sure that she could find her way back. Thus, her arrival at the field was not "by chance." Even so, Rashi adds that Ruth's appearance at the exact part of the field owned by Boaz was coincidental.

ב:ד וְהִנֵּה־בֹעַז בָּא מִבֵּית לֶחֶם וַיֹּאמֶר לַקּוֹצְרִים יְהוָה עִמָּכֶם וַיֹּאמְרוּ לוֹ יְבָרֶכְךָ יְהוָה:

**2:4** AT THAT MOMENT, BOAZ CAME FROM BETHLEHEM. HE GREETED THE REAPERS, "MAY *ADONAI* BE WITH YOU." THEY REPLIED, "MAY *ADONAI* BLESS YOU."

As seen in various places in the Torah, the Hebrew word *v'hinei* (literally, "behold") may suggest something important that concludes a series of events of lesser importance. Here Ruth finds the right field, follows the reapers, and finishes gleaning the fields just at the moment that Boaz arrives. Her timing seems perfect. She is a woman who knows what she wants and how to get it.

In order to avoid any hint of anthropomorphism, the *Targum* changes Boaz's comments to the workers to "May the word of *Adonai* be your support." It does, however, have the reapers respond, "May *Adonai* bless you." Ibn Ezra explains Boaz's words to the reapers as "*Adonai* should assist you [in your work]." He explains their response to Boaz as in keeping with the way that laborers might respond to their employer: "May *Adonai* give a blessing in the harvest." This is consistent with the comments of both Rashi and Ibn Ezra on Numbers 6:24, where the Priestly Benediction appears, in which they read the expression "May *Adonai* bless you" as related to property and wealth. The word *b'rachah* has that meaning of "gift" in Genesis 33:11, Joshua 15:19, and elsewhere.

ב:ה וַיֹּאמֶר בֹּעַז לְנַעֲרוֹ הַנִּצָּב עַל־הַקּוֹצְרִים לְמִי הַנַּעֲרָה הַזֹּאת:

**2:5** BOAZ SAID TO HIS SERVANT WHO SUPERVISED THE REAPERS, "WHO IS THAT WOMAN?"

It is clear that Ruth has caught Boaz's attention. Perhaps he is surprised to see a woman in the field. Maybe her looks defy her mode of dress. One implication of this verse is that Boaz is struck by Ruth's beauty and is attracted to her.

Although the Hebrew in the last clause suggests possession (literally, "To whom does that woman belong?"), our translation follows the *Targum*, which understands the question in terms of identity, that is, "To which nation does that woman belong?" Thus, we have translated it into a more comfortable contemporary idiom, "Who is that woman?"

The *Targum* explains that *hanitzav* in this context (literally, "the one standing") means "the one that Boaz has appointed as leader." Rashi, embarrassed by the literal meaning of Boaz's question, asks somewhat rhetorically, "Was it Boaz's habit to inquire about women?" He then explains that Boaz was intrigued by Ruth's wisdom and modesty, which he surmised because she gleaned two ears at a time rather than three. Also she stood to glean ears that were still standing, but she gleaned fallen ears while sitting so that she did not bend over in an immodest manner.

There are two explanations for Boaz's question in Ibn Ezra's interpretation. Either he wondered if she was a married woman or he noticed that her clothing exposed her Moabite origins.

ב:ו וַיַּעַן הַנַּעַר הַנִּצָּב עַל־הַקּוֹצְרִים וַיֹּאמַר נַעֲרָה מוֹאֲבִיָּה הִיא הַשָּׁבָה עִם־נָעֳמִי מִשְּׂדֵה מוֹאָב:

2:6 THE SERVANT SUPERVISING THE REAPERS ANSWERED, "SHE IS A MOABITE WOMAN, WHO RETURNED WITH NAOMI FROM THE COUNTRY OF MOAB.

It is unclear why Ruth's Moabite origins are repeated once again. The emphasis seems to stress that despite her origins, David and the messianic line could emerge from such a woman. Pointing attention to her foreignness also makes her actions and those of Boaz seem all the more remarkable. In addition, the author includes Ruth in Naomi's "return." They are now a unit.

The *Targum* is not satisfied with the servant's answer, especially since Ruth is from Moab, and so adds the word *v'itgaarat* (and she converted to Judaism) to the servant's response.

ב:ז וַתֹּאמֶר אֲלַקֳטָה־נָּא וְאָסַפְתִּי בָעֳמָרִים אַחֲרֵי הַקּוֹצְרִים וַתָּבוֹא וַתַּעֲמוֹד מֵאָז הַבֹּקֶר וְעַד־עַתָּה זֶה שִׁבְתָּהּ הַבַּיִת מְעָט:

2:7 "SHE SAID, 'PLEASE LET ME GLEAN AND GATHER SOME SHEAVES FOLLOWING THE REAPERS.' FROM THE TIME SHE CAME IN THE MORNING UNTIL NOW, SHE HAS BEEN STANDING, RARELY SITTING IN THE HUT."

The servant provides Boaz with more information than requested. Clearly, the servant is also intrigued by Ruth and her unusual habits. In this translation, we have followed Ibn Ezra's understanding that the structure called *habayit* (literally, "the house"), used by the workers for rest and shade from the sun, is *k'mo sukkah*, "like a hut." The servant's statement that Ruth has rarely sat in the hut is a testament to both her work ethic and her righteousness, for it could have been seen as socially inappropriate for her to lie down and rest among the male workers. The impression is that she was there to work, not to socialize. For the *Targum*, the implication of the verse is that Ruth got to work even earlier than the servant suggests in his report to Boaz. It translates "in the morning" as *mikdam tzafrah,* "even before morning."

Perhaps it is Rashi's concern for Ruth's modesty that motivated him to read this verse as Ruth speaking to herself rather than to the supervisor. He sees the fulfillment of two different mitzvot in Ruth's request. "Let me glean" refers to the mitzvah of *leket* (gleaning), and "gather" is a reference to *shich-chah,* "that which is forgotten" in the field.

Ibn Ezra understands "she came" and "she has been standing" as indications that Ruth is only interested in doing her work and nothing else. Therefore, her beauty would not cause suspicion.

בַּח וַיֹּאמֶר בֹּעַז אֶל־רוּת הֲלוֹא שָׁמַעַתְּ בִּתִּי אַל־תֵּלְכִי לִלְקֹט בְּשָׂדֶה אַחֵר וְגַם לֹא תַעֲבוּרִי מִזֶּה וְכֹה תִדְבָּקִין עִם־נַעֲרֹתָי:

**2:8** THEN BOAZ SAID TO RUTH, "MY DAUGHTER, LISTEN TO ME. DON'T GO GLEANING IN ANY OTHER FIELD. DON'T LEAVE THIS PLACE, BUT STICK CLOSE TO MY FEMALE FIELDWORKERS.

Boaz is motivated to offer Ruth all she wants. He doesn't want her to leave, but he also doesn't want to be too aggressive in his behavior toward her.

While it is introduced with a negative particle *halo,* Boaz's statement often has the sense of being a positive imperative (see Genesis 20:5 and I Kings 1:11). Hence, we have taken the idiomatic meaning of *halo shamaat* (literally, "have you not heard?") and translated it as "listen to me."

The *Targum* understands "don't leave this place" as a reference to Ruth's newly chosen identity, meaning "don't leave to join another people."

Ibn Ezra takes note of the grammar once again. Though he offers no explanation, Ibn Ezra comments that the word *taavuri* (leave) has an unusual—though not totally uncommon—vowel in the word. In the place of *o,* we find *u.* Additionally, he remarks that the *nun* at the end of *tidbakin* (stick close) is extraneous.

ב:ט עֵינַ֜יִךְ בַּשָּׂדֶ֣ה אֲשֶׁר־יִקְצֹרוּן֮ וְהָלַ֣כְתְּ אַחֲרֵיהֶן֒ הֲל֧וֹא צִוִּ֣יתִי אֶת־
הַנְּעָרִ֖ים לְבִלְתִּ֣י נָגְעֵ֑ךְ וְצָמִ֗ת וְהָלַכְתְּ֙ אֶל־הַכֵּלִ֔ים וְשָׁתִ֕ית מֵאֲשֶׁ֥ר
יִשְׁאֲב֖וּן הַנְּעָרִֽים:

**2:9** "KEEP YOUR EYES IN THE FIELD WHERE THEY WILL BE
REAPING AND FOLLOW AFTER THEM. I HAVE ORDERED
THE YOUNG MALE WORKERS NOT TO BOTHER YOU.
WHEN YOU GET THIRSTY, GO TO THE [WATER] POTS
AND DRINK WHATEVER [WATER] THE YOUNG MEN HAVE
DRAWN."

While it appears that Boaz is altruistically being protective of Ruth, he also wants to
make it clear to all his workers that this is no ordinary female worker. They are to help
her but in no way to be under the impression that she is available to them. His actions
indicate to his workers that she is special to him. Moreover, he tells them that they are
responsible for her well-being. As a symbol of life, water reflects that concern.

Since the Hebrew text merely has *einayich* (your eyes), idiomatically translated
here as "keep your eyes," the *Targum* adds *tehay mistackla* (keep looking) to explain
"your eyes."

Rashi adds "don't be embarrassed" to "when you get thirsty" to amplify his
understanding of the verse. Ibn Ezra makes yet another grammatical note—*tzamit*
(you get thirsty) comes from the root *tz-m-a*—but he offers no explanation.

ב:י וַתִּפֹּל֙ עַל־פָּנֶ֔יהָ וַתִּשְׁתַּ֖חוּ אָ֑רְצָה וַתֹּ֣אמֶר אֵלָ֗יו מַדּ֩וּעַ֩ מָצָ֨אתִי חֵ֤ן
בְּעֵינֶ֙יךָ֙ לְהַכִּירֵ֔נִי וְאָנֹכִ֖י נָכְרִיָּֽה:

**2:10** SHE PROSTRATED HERSELF FACEDOWN UPON THE
GROUND AND SAID TO HIM, "WHY HAVE I FOUND
SUCH FAVOR IN YOUR SIGHT THAT EVEN THOUGH I AM
A FOREIGNER, YOU PAY ATTENTION TO ME?"

This is a significant act of humility, but it can also be read in a contemporary idiom as
"she threw herself at his feet." The sexual tension between Ruth and Boaz begins to
elevate as their relationship quickly builds. By her comment, we see that Ruth
continues to explore her new identity within the people and the Land of Israel.

The *Targum* expands Ruth's statement "I am a foreigner" by adding "I am from a
foreign people, from the daughters of Moab, from a people that is not worth entering
the community of *Adonai*." By disparaging the people of Moab, the *Targum* attempts
to raise the status of the people of Israel, a common practice by those who are
uncomfortable with newcomers to the community, especially non-Jews.

**ב:יא** וַיַּעַן בֹּעַז וַיֹּאמֶר לָהּ הֻגֵּד הֻגַּד לִי כֹּל אֲשֶׁר־עָשִׂית אֶת־חֲמוֹתֵךְ
אַחֲרֵי מוֹת אִישֵׁךְ וַתַּעַזְבִי אָבִיךְ וְאִמֵּךְ וְאֶרֶץ מוֹלַדְתֵּךְ וַתֵּלְכִי
אֶל־עַם אֲשֶׁר לֹא־יָדַעַתְּ תְּמוֹל שִׁלְשׁוֹם:

2:11 BOAZ REPLIED, "I WAS TOLD OF ALL THAT YOU DID FOR
YOUR MOTHER-IN-LAW AFTER THE DEATH OF YOUR
HUSBAND, HOW YOU LEFT YOUR FATHER AND MOTHER
AND THE LAND OF YOUR BIRTH, AND HOW YOU WENT
TO A PEOPLE WHOM YOU HAD NOT PREVIOUSLY
KNOWN.

The *Targum* understands this verse to reflect the idea that Boaz was informed by the
Sages that the prohibition against Moabites entering the Israelite community applied
only to men, not women. Furthermore, he was informed by prophecy that prophets
and kings would descend from Ruth because of her conversion.

Ibn Ezra expands the phrase "whom you had not previously known" with the
words "to dwell among them."

The reader has no way of knowing how Boaz learned about Ruth. Perhaps his
knowledge of Ruth's actions, which he clearly considers admirable, emerges from the
"chatter" described in 1:19. The author continues to emphasize Ruth's strength, what
it took to do what she did. With or without the experience of death, it takes a great
deal to cast one's lot with a people that one was not born into.

**ב:יב** יְשַׁלֵּם יְהוָה פָּעֳלֵךְ וּתְהִי מַשְׂכֻּרְתֵּךְ שְׁלֵמָה מֵעִם יְהוָה אֱלֹהֵי
יִשְׂרָאֵל אֲשֶׁר־בָּאת לַחֲסוֹת תַּחַת־כְּנָפָיו:

2:12 "MAY *ADONAI* REWARD YOU FOR ALL YOU HAVE DONE.
MAY YOU RECEIVE PAYMENT IN FULL FROM *ADONAI*,
THE GOD OF ISRAEL IN WHOSE PRESENCE YOU HAVE
TAKEN REFUGE."

Ruth's actions are meritorious. By placing such words in Boaz's mouth, the author tells
the reader that *Adonai*, the God of Israel, approves of Ruth's actions. As one who
obviously believes in God, Boaz makes it clear—through his own blessing—that Ruth,
and others like her, should be welcomed into the Jewish community. Moreover, they
are deserving of our praise.

In its translation, the *Targum* adds "in this world" to "May *Adonai* reward you" and
"in the world-to-come" after "payment in full." It avoids the possibility of anthropomorphism by adding "beneath the shadow of the Divine Presence [*Shechinah*] of
glory" after "whose presence" (literally, "beneath His divine wings"). It then adds

"because of that merit you will be saved from the judgment of *Geihinom*, so that your portion will be with Sarah, Rebekah, Rachel, and Leah."

Ibn Ezra claims that *maskoret* (payment) has the same meaning as *matkonet* (measurement), as in Exodus 5:8.

ב:יג וַתֹּאמֶר אֶמְצָא־חֵן בְּעֵינֶיךָ אֲדֹנִי כִּי נִחַמְתָּנִי וְכִי דִבַּרְתָּ עַל־לֵב שִׁפְחָתֶךָ וְאָנֹכִי לֹא אֶהְיֶה כְּאַחַת שִׁפְחֹתֶיךָ:

2:13 [THEN] SHE SAID, "SIR, EVEN THOUGH I AM NOT AS IMPORTANT AS ONE OF YOUR FEMALE FIELDWORKERS, YOU DO ME A GREAT KINDNESS TO SPEAK TO ME IN SUCH A SWEET WAY AND TO GIVE ME SUCH COMFORT."

Ruth remains uncomfortable in the midst of such praise. Perhaps it is genuine modesty, or maybe she is trying to impress Boaz with a self-effacing posture. While she appreciates his act of kindness to her, Boaz's female fieldworkers deserve his concern as well. After all, they labor daily in the sun for him, whereas Ruth has just arrived on the scene, seeking only sustenance for herself and Naomi.

It is often difficult to translate Hebrew idioms into contemporary English. We have thus translated *emtza chein b'einecha* (literally, "I will find favor in your eyes") as "you do me a great kindness." And we have rendered *dibarta al lev shifchatecha* (literally, "You have spoken to/on the heart of your servant girls") as "to speak to me in such a sweet way." Both translations seem to fit the spirit of the verse. We have followed Rashi in his addition of "important" to the phrase "as one of your female fieldworkers."

The *Targum* adds "to prepare me to be worthy [to enter] the community of God" after "you do me a great kindness" and the phrase "to promise me that I will inherit the world-to-come by this righteous act, even though I am not as worthy as one of your female fieldworkers to receive a portion in the world-to-come." Where Rashi inserts the word "important" in his explanation of the phrase "as important as one of your female fieldworkers," Ibn Ezra places the word "fitting."

ב:יד וַיֹּאמֶר לָה בֹעַז לְעֵת הָאֹכֶל גֹּשִׁי הֲלֹם וְאָכַלְתְּ מִן־הַלֶּחֶם וְטָבַלְתְּ
פִּתֵּךְ בַּחֹמֶץ וַתֵּשֶׁב מִצַּד הַקּוֹצְרִים וַיִּצְבָּט־לָהּ קָלִי וַתֹּאכַל
וַתִּשְׂבַּע וַתֹּתַר:

**2:14** BOAZ SAID TO HER, "WHEN IT COMES TIME TO EAT, COME OVER HERE AND HAVE A MEAL. YOU CAN DIP YOUR BREAD IN THE VINEGAR." SHE SAT DOWN NEXT TO THE REAPERS, AND HE OFFERED HER SOME ROASTED GRAIN. SHE ATE UNTIL SHE HAD HAD ENOUGH AND LEFT SOME OVER.

As both Rashi and Ibn Ezra note, *vayitzbot* (from the root *tz-b-t*) occurs only in this verse, making the meaning of the word somewhat unclear. Koehler-Baumgartner (p. 997) translate the word as "pick up and offer," which has influenced this translation. The *Targum* uses the word *v'oshit* (he stretched out). For the *Targum*, more than "bread" was dipped "in the vinegar." Though the author may have intended to imply something sexual, the *Targum* expands Boaz's generosity, imagining that he tells Ruth to "dip your food into a dish that has been cooked in vinegar." Both Rashi and Ibn Ezra explain the "dipping of food into vinegar" as the reapers' way of dealing with the heat of harvest time. The sexual intimations of the interchange are unmistakable though and give a hint of what is to come.

ב:טו וַתָּקָם לְלַקֵּט וַיְצַו בֹּעַז אֶת־נְעָרָיו לֵאמֹר גַּם בֵּין הָעֳמָרִים תְּלַקֵּט
וְלֹא תַכְלִימוּהָ:

**2:15** WHEN SHE GOT UP AGAIN TO GLEAN, BOAZ TOLD HIS YOUNG MALE WORKERS, "LET HER GLEAN EVEN AMONG THE SHEAVES AND DON'T YELL AT HER.

The text suggests that gleaning followed the harvesting but was to cease when the grain was stacked. Boaz here instructs his workers to let Ruth glean wherever she wants and not to reproach her for doing so. Although the *Targum* translates *v'lo tachlimuha* (don't embarrass) as *v'la tachsifehnah* (don't put to shame), we have elected to translate the words in a more idiomatic way: "don't yell at her." If Ruth were simply a poor woman, collecting gleanings from the field, she would not be permitted to take grain from the already harvested stacks of grain. Were she to do so, undoubtedly Boaz's workers would reprimand her, and such scolding would embarrass her. It would also embarrass Boaz, since he had given Ruth free reign to take her fill from the harvest. If Boaz is attracted to Ruth, he wants to make sure that she is treated well, even if he has not yet expressed his feelings toward her.

ב:טז וְגַם שֹׁל־תָּשֹׁלּוּ לָהּ מִן־הַצְּבָתִים וַעֲזַבְתֶּם וְלִקְּטָה וְלֹא תִגְעֲרוּ־בָהּ׃

**2:16** "Do something more: pull out some stalks of wheat from the heap and leave them for her to glean. Don't holler at her!"

The use of the root *sh-l-l* to mean "pulling out stalks" occurs only here in the *Tanach*. Such a definition suggests that the verb is a homonym of the root *sh-l-l*, which means "to plunder, rob" (cf. Koehler-Baumgartner, p. 1531).

Since it occurs in only one place in the *Tanach*, this verb poses a problem for the *Targum*, Rashi, and Ibn Ezra. While the *Targum* understands the verb *sh-l-l* as "to leave," Rashi takes it to mean "pretend to forget" or somehow related to "become detached" (from the root *n-sh-l*, "slip off," as in Deuteronomy 28:40). Ibn Ezra contends that the word refers to either "plunder" or "err." With each variant reading the verse means something different. Each one implies a different attitude toward Ruth by Boaz as reflected in Boaz's instructions to his male fieldworkers. The behavior implicit in the *Targum*'s translation is straightforward, "Just *leave* some stalks," and Ruth will be able to glean an abundant amount of grain. In Rashi's translation, the workers are to "pretend to forget" the sheaves so that Ruth does not realize that they are following Boaz's orders. With Ibn Ezra, the actions of the servants would be a simple mistake.

ב:יז וַתְּלַקֵּט בַּשָּׂדֶה עַד־הָעָרֶב וַתַּחְבֹּט אֵת אֲשֶׁר־לִקֵּטָה וַיְהִי כְּאֵיפָה שְׂעֹרִים׃

**2:17** So she gleaned in the field until evening. She beat out the grain she had gleaned, and it amounted to about an ephah of barley.

Boaz is not providing Ruth with prepared food or even processed grain, which he could do if he so chose. Instead, he wants to preserve her dignity by not so explicitly showing his interest in her to others, or by simply giving her a handout. So she takes the stalks of grain and grinds them into flour. This proves to Boaz the industrious nature of her character. Nevertheless, Boaz provides her with what seems to be an abundant amount.

An ephah is a measurement used for grain, probably about half a bushel or the equivalent of five gallons of liquid measure. The *Targum* explains it in terms of another measurement used for grain: an ephah is three *seahs*, another obscure measurement. In either case, the implication seems to be that it was a lot of barley.

In his comment on the verse, Ibn Ezra recounts an interesting question and offers some peculiar answers. He had apparently been asked what the point was of the statement "about an ephah of barley." He answered that the text merely reported what happened. But Ibn Ezra's response did not satisfy the questioner. So the questioner proceeded to offer his own answers: it was to teach that Ruth prophetically learned that one of the sons she would conceive would erect a pillar in the name of her husband and that the ephah (the numerical value of which is ninety-six) is an indicator that ninety-six pomegranates would be placed on that pillar. Moreover, "barley" (s'orim) suggests the word sei-ar (hair). It was thus understood to predict the death of Ruth's descendant Absalom, whose very long hair (II Samuel 14:25–26) caused his death (II Samuel 18:9–15).

ב:יח וַתִּשָּׂא וַתָּבוֹא הָעִיר וַתֵּרֶא חֲמוֹתָהּ אֵת אֲשֶׁר־לִקֵּטָה וַתּוֹצֵא וַתִּתֶּן־לָהּ אֵת אֲשֶׁר־הוֹתִרָה מִשָּׂבְעָהּ:

2:18 SHE LIFTED IT UP AND WENT BACK TO THE CITY. WHEN HER MOTHER-IN-LAW SAW ALL THAT SHE HAD GLEANED, AND WHEN SHE TOOK OUT AND GAVE HER WHAT HAD REMAINED AFTER HAVING EATEN HER FILL...

The author does not provide us with many details such as where or how Ruth prepared the grain. It seems that she carried it back to the city on her own. Ruth must have stopped along the way to bake some bread or prepare the flour in some way for eating, as well.

The *Targum* fills in what seems to be missing in the verse by providing the reader with what Ruth took out (mezonah, "food") and from what she took it out (tarmil, "a bag").

ב:יט וַתֹּאמֶר לָהּ חֲמוֹתָהּ אֵיפֹה לִקַּטְתְּ הַיּוֹם וְאָנָה עָשִׂית יְהִי מַכִּירֵךְ בָּרוּךְ וַתַּגֵּד לַחֲמוֹתָהּ אֵת אֲשֶׁר־עָשְׂתָה עִמּוֹ וַתֹּאמֶר שֵׁם הָאִישׁ אֲשֶׁר עָשִׂיתִי עִמּוֹ הַיּוֹם בֹּעַז:

2:19 HER MOTHER-IN-LAW ASKED HER, "WHERE DID YOU GLEAN TODAY? WHERE DID YOU WORK? MAY THE ONE WHO NOTICED YOU BE BLESSED." RUTH TOLD HER MOTHER-IN-LAW FOR WHOM SHE HAD WORKED AND SAID, "BOAZ IS THE NAME OF THE MAN I WORKED FOR."

Naomi is clearly astonished by Ruth's accomplishments. Between Naomi's queries and then her blessing for the not yet identified individual who showed her kindness, there must have been some exchange between the two of them. It is almost as if the third line in the verse should come earlier. In any case, this verse and those that follow show the equivalent of excited chatter between Naomi and Ruth.

While the *Targum* simply translates the verse in its plainest form, Rashi explains that ''the one who noticed'' is the owner of the field.

ב:כ וַתֹּאמֶר נָעֳמִי לְכַלָּתָהּ בָּרוּךְ הוּא לַיהֹוָה אֲשֶׁר לֹא־עָזַב חַסְדּוֹ
אֶת־הַחַיִּים וְאֶת־הַמֵּתִים וַתֹּאמֶר לָהּ נָעֳמִי קָרוֹב לָנוּ הָאִישׁ
מִגֹּאֲלֵנוּ הוּא:

**2:20** NAOMI THEN SAID TO HER DAUGHTER-IN-LAW, ''THE ONE WHO HAS NOT KEPT BACK HIS CONTINUOUS LOVE FROM THE LIVING OR THE DEAD IS BLESSED OF *ADONAI*.'' SHE CONTINUED, ''THE MAN IS A RELATIVE, ONE BOUND TO REDEEM US.''

Perhaps Naomi is repeating a proverb and assigning it to Boaz or her reaction is a reflection of her emotions. In any case, she identifies Boaz as a relative responsible to redeem them. While Ruth may have thought that Boaz was just being generous—and even attracted to her—she has realized that he might have been acting out of a sense of responsibility to her family.

The redeemer mentioned here is the one who will marry the widow of a relative. In an effort to avoid anthropomorphism, the *Targum* inserts *mepum kedusha dadonai* (from the mouth of the holiness of *Adonai*) alongside the reference to God in the verse. Rashi understands ''with the living'' to mean that God provides for the living and is involved in taking care of the dead. For Ibn Ezra, ''the dead'' refers to Elimelech and his sons, and ''the living'' is a reference to Naomi and Ruth. Ibn Ezra denies, however, that the *go-eil* (redeemer) here mentioned is the same as the *yavam* (the husband's brother [Deuteronomy 25:5, 25:7]). While he offers no specific suggestion, he argues that what is described here is some other kind of redemption.

ב:כא וַתֹּאמֶר רוּת הַמּוֹאֲבִיָּה גַּם כִּי־אָמַר אֵלַי עִם־הַנְּעָרִים אֲשֶׁר־לִי
תִּדְבָּקִין עַד אִם־כִּלּוּ אֵת כָּל־הַקָּצִיר אֲשֶׁר־לִי:

**2:21** RUTH THE MOABITE SAID, ''HE ALSO TOLD ME TO STICK CLOSE TO HIS MALE WORKERS UNTIL THEY HAVE FINISHED THE HARVEST.''

The author once again reminds us of Ruth's origins. Perhaps the author is identifying her in much the same style as other biblical authors employ, but it seems to be reminding us that while she was once a Moabite, forbidden to Israel, she has been fully accepted into the community. It is possible that such identification is relevant to the author's attempt to impugn Ruth's character.

To make the English translation smoother, we have translated *han'arim asher li* (literally, "my young men") as "his male workers." Such a translation allows us to maintain some of the sexual tension implicit in the issue of men and women working together, which is a focus of this section of the text. We have also translated *kol hakatzir asher li* (literally, "all my harvest") as "the harvest."

וַתֹּאמֶר נָעֳמִי אֶל־רוּת כַּלָּתָהּ טוֹב בִּתִּי כִּי תֵצְאִי עִם־נַעֲרוֹתָיו **ב:כב**
וְלֹא יִפְגְּעוּ־בָךְ בְּשָׂדֶה אַחֵר:

**2:22** NAOMI SAID TO RUTH, HER DAUGHTER-IN-LAW, "IT WOULD BE BEST IF YOU WENT OUT TO WORK WITH HIS YOUNG WOMEN AND NOT BE BOTHERED IN SOME OTHER FIELD."

Ruth assumes that Boaz told her to stay close to the male fieldworkers loyal to him as a way of protecting her. But Naomi is afraid that the men might try to take advantage of her, thinking that it is safer to work among women than men. Naomi might also be trying to protect Ruth's reputation, fearing that community members might think her immodest for working among men. Whatever the case, the image of young men and women working alongside one another in the field connotes a sense that this was a sexually charged situation.

Ibn Ezra, picking up on the sexual undercurrents of the story, notes that Naomi's advice to Ruth is about avoiding the male workers in the field.

וַתִּדְבַּק בְּנַעֲרוֹת בֹּעַז לְלַקֵּט עַד־כְּלוֹת קְצִיר־הַשְּׂעֹרִים וּקְצִיר **ב:כג**
הַחִטִּים וַתֵּשֶׁב אֶת־חֲמוֹתָהּ:

**2:23** SO RUTH STUCK CLOSE TO THE YOUNG WOMEN WHO WORKED FOR BOAZ, TO GLEAN UNTIL BOTH THE BARLEY HARVEST AND THE WHEAT HARVEST WERE COMPLETED. THEN SHE LIVED WITH HER MOTHER-IN-LAW.

It seems that Ruth followed her mother-in-law's advice, a manifestation of Ruth's own modesty and deference to her mother-in-law. The sense of the verse is that she went to the field, gleaned, did not fraternize with any of the workers—male or female—and went home to spend time with Naomi. This verse also offers appropriate closure to the chapter.

The *Biblia Hebraica* (p. 1198), considered a critical edition of the Bible because it takes into consideration various standard manuscripts of the Bible, notes that two variant manuscripts read *vatashov el chamota* as the last three words of the verse rather than *vateishev et chamotah*. Such a reading would change the verse from "she lived with her mother-in-law" to "she returned to her mother-in-law." While such a reading requires a change of vowels in one word and a letter in another, a common practice among some critical scholars, it makes the verse more comprehensible. By translating *vateishev et* as *vetayvat im,* the *Targum* maintains the sense of the verse as we have it: "and she lived with." Ibn Ezra too struggles with the meaning of the verse, arguing that *et* can have the meaning of *im* (with).

## Nahshon ben Aminadav

When the Israelites were poised to cross the Red Sea following their exodus from Egypt, the Israelites were afraid to enter the water. Moses did not know how to persuade them, and the Egyptian armies were in hot pursuit. According to a midrash (Babylonian Talmud, *Sotah* 36b), Nahshon ben Aminadav of the tribe of Judah was first to enter the water. It was only after he entered the sea, having put his life in God's hands, that the waters parted. While Moses prayed to God for guidance, Nahshon jumped to action. It was this action that made the miracle happen.

## Gleanings (Leket)

*Leket* is one of three parts of the harvest, along with *shich-chah* (forgotten sheaves) and *pei-ah* (corners of the field), which together are known as *matnot aniyim* (gifts to the poor). *Leket* refers specifically to stalks that are dropped by the harvester that may not be retrieved. Instead, they are left behind for the poor to collect (see Leviticus 19:9–10). While the technical term is different (*peret*), the same holds true for grapes that have fallen during the harvest. The episode of gleaning retold in this chapter, where gleaners actually follow the reapers, awaiting the opportunity to collect the gleanings, is the best known in the Bible. Since gleaning is limited to grainfields, orchards, and vineyards, the same principle does not apply to vegetable gardens.

## Forgotten Sheaves (Shich-chah)

*Shich-chah* refers to sheaves that harvesters overlook and leave in the field. They may not return to retrieve them. Instead, these sheaves, like gleanings, must be left for the poor (see Deuteronomy 24:19). While the Bible refers only to cut sheaves, the Rabbis extend this principle of social justice to include uncut grain and trees that had been overlooked as well (Jerusalem Talmud, *Pei-ah* 6:7, 7:1).

## World-to-Come

The eschatological concept of a world-to-come (*olam haba*) developed during the period of the Second Temple. This concept was expanded upon in subsequent rabbinic literature. While the term *olam* originally was related to space, it later took on the dimension of time. Jewish tradition suggests that a major event, such as the Day of Judgment, would bring this world to an end and usher in the next world, that is, the world-to-come. "Heaven" and "paradise" are terms used interchangeably to define *olam haba*. However, some make a distinction between the temporary place where souls reside prior to final judgment and the "other world" where the departed souls of "good" people permanently reside.

## Geihinom

The Jewish version of "hell," *Geihinom*, or Gehenna, literally refers to a valley south of Jerusalem on one of the borders between the territories of Judah and Benjamin (cf. Joshua 15:8, 18:16). During the time of the monarchy, it was a site associated with a cult that burned children, a practice condemned by Jeremiah. In the rabbinic period, the name is used to refer to the place of torment reserved for the wicked after death. It stands in contradistinction to *Gan Eden*, the "Garden of Eden," which in rabbinic literature became known as the place of reward for the righteous. In the Bible these two names are never used to connote the abode of souls after death. Yet, in rabbinic literature such references abound: according to the Babylonian Talmud, *P'sachim* 54a, *Geihinom* and *Gan Eden* existed even before the world was created; in the midrash to Psalm 50:12, *Geihinom* is at the left hand of God and *Gan Eden* at God's right.

## Redeeming of Relatives

The role of the *go-eil* (redeemer) seems to have developed over time. It has to do with somehow redeeming a relative, the next of kin. One may redeem a relative by paying off a debt whereby he sold himself into slavery (Leviticus 25:48) or may buy back a relative's home for similar reasons (Leviticus 25:25). The *go-eil* also was the one who avenged the death of a relative (Numbers 35:12); this redeemer is frequently referred to as a "blood avenger." God is the ultimate next of kin and is the *go-eil* (redeemer) of the Jewish people (see Exodus 6:6; Job 19:25). In the case of divine redemption, the work of the *go-eil* can be political or social, as in the case of the Exodus from Egypt, or can include total cosmic transformation in the form of messianic redemption.

# GLEANINGS

## *New Definitions*

Jews-by-choice present a new paradigm for all Jews. In terms of ethnicity, Irish-American Jews, African-American Jews, Italian-American Jews, and Japanese-American Jews are redefining the Jewish nose, the Jewish menu, the Jewish name. And for liberal Jews, converts pose an even more fundamental challenge. The Jew-by-choice embodies the fact that it is no longer possible to simply *be* Jewish in an unselfconscious, effortless ethnic way. An authentic sense of being Jewish—of Jewish*ness*—is available only to those who live as Jews, who *do* Jewish. Fortunately, the list of Jewish things to do is enormous and its variety (study, prayer, affiliation, ritual practice, social activism, music, hospitality, philanthropy, cooking) encourages individuality as much as it fosters community.

In a world where Jews participate fully in the free marketplace of ideas, in a time when ghetto walls and anti-Semitic quotas do not exist, in a time of spiritual hunger, converts are a contemporary model of Jewish identity. From synagogue pulpits of every denomination, the message has been repeated so often it has become a truism, "Whether we are born Jewish or have converted to Judaism, we are all Jews-by-choice."

Anita Diamant, *Choosing a Jewish Life: A Handbook for People Converting to Judaism and for Their Family and Friends* (New York: Schocken Books, 1997), 23

## *Modesty Is Expressed in Many Fashions*

No one could argue with the principle of "preserving the integrity of the individual," and no one would disagree with the perception that our personhood is *kadosh* [holy]. The problem arises when we ask more specific questions about *tzniut* [modesty] as a life mode, as "the bedrock of Judaism." What is really meant by modesty in dress? Does it mean that I should not wear a pants suit to work? Does it mean that I should not appear on a public beach in a bathing suit? Does it mean that I should cover my hair? Can I wear sleeveless dresses?... Is my body less *kadosh* in a bathing suit than in a long dress? For me the question is not one of modesty in dress but rather appropriateness in dress....

Do "permissive clothes" somehow cause permissive sexual relationships? Is the world we live in really a situation where "our bodies, and the precious inner jewels of our personality, are open to all comers"? I don't think so (and I live in California!). In the area of sexuality, as in the area of dress, the major issue is one of appropriate response. It is appropriate in certain instances to "open up" emotionally, to touch or kiss or be physically intimate. In other situations it is inappropriate. Who is to judge?

Each individual should be encouraged to make his/her own decisions based on his/her own understanding of the sanctity of personhood.

Laura Geller, "Modesty Is Expressed in Many Fashions,"
*Sh'ma: A Journal of Jewish Responsibility* 9, no. 162 (November 24, 1978): 11

## Today's Ruth

Taking Ruth's journey as our guide, we imagine that love would be there from the beginning. Love, and an ounce of rebellion and risk. Today's Ruth would know that she was willing to leave her family and homeland, to set off on an uncharted journey alongside her beloved. Probably, such a bold person had already rejected aspects of her upbringing, seeking alternatives to the familiar.

If Ruth's journey begins in love, it deepens with knowledge. To become attached to a homeland and a people requires learning their language, history, culture and traditions. Today's Ruth would study Hebrew and Judaism as part of her people's heritage. She would learn how to read the news as a Jew, seeing the world afresh. She would come to appreciate the Sabbath, as a day for rest, contemplation, family. She would seek out other Jews, joining organizations that shared her commitments and welcomed her.

Gradually, as her perceptions, experiences, language and culture changed, she would come to wrestle with the God of Israel. Undoubtedly, those festivals that celebrate a people's traditions, such as Hanukkah and Pesah, would appeal more than those that focus on God's power and glory, such as Shavuot and Yom Kippur. As for critical events in the life cycle—from birth, through bar mitzvah, to marriage—today's Ruth would see them as part of her culture. She would want to participate fully in each.

Should Jews welcome today's Ruth? I think they should. Barring her from religious activities in synagogues creates a hierarchy that elevates rabbinic attitudes toward boundaries over folk traditions. We need to recognize how Jews as a transnational people consistently violated borders established by gentiles. Rather than imitating gentile practices segregating Jews, we should work to reconnect peoplehood and faith.

Deborah Dash Moore, "Today's Ruth," *Sh'ma: A Journal of
Jewish Responsibility* 30, no. 565 (October 1999): 6

## On Giving to Others

People can give either time or money or both to causes they care about. There is an extraordinary value in giving time, in being of service, in giving what is really a piece of oneself. It sends a powerful message to the people being helped that someone cares enough to be there with them and share in their work. A group of volunteers, helping to dig house foundations in El Salvador and finding themselves not particularly skilled for the task, were asked if it might not be more efficient for them to just send money to the project. The Director said, "Yes, but it would not send the same spiritual message."

Being of service also has the power to transform the giver. To travel to Honduras with a group to help rebuild homes lost in a hurricane, to stand shoulder-to-shoulder with the people who live in that home, has the power to take you outside yourself, to change your view of the world, to help you identify with the other. So, too, can helping another person become a reader or sharing your professional skills—in nutrition or spreadsheets or management—with people who are eager to learn. It also helps you see yourself as someone with the power to make a difference in the world, a person with agency, a person who can assume responsibility to address the challenges of our time.

Our tradition recognizes the importance of this giving when it teaches that our lives get meaning not from what we say or what we believe but from the deeds we do. Or, as Gandhi said, "You must be the change you wish to see in the world."

When we send our volunteers out as individuals or in groups to be of service to people in all corners of the globe we share with them an observation attributed to an Australian aborigine woman: "If you have come here to help me, you are wasting your time. But if you have come here because your liberation is bound up with mine, then let us get to work."

Ruth Messinger, in *Kolot: Valuing Giving* (Wyncote, PA: Kolot:
The Center for Jewish Women's and Gender Studies, 2003), 52–53

## *Holy Economics*

If Ruth came to America today, what would happen? Would she be admitted at the border? Would she have to show a "green card" before she could get a job gleaning at any farm, restaurant, or hospital? Would she face contempt because she spent a night with Boaz on the threshing floor?

Through the book of Ruth, the Bible affirms that in a decent society everyone is entitled to decent work for a decent income. Everyone—even, or especially, a despised immigrant. Everyone—not just 95 percent of the people.

Ruth was entitled not only to a job, but to respect. Boaz reminded his workers: No name-calling, no sexual harassment.

And she, as well as Boaz, was entitled to Sabbath: time off for rest, reflection, celebration, love. She was entitled to "be" as well as to "do."

How do we know that Ruth was entitled to rest, as well as to work at a living wage? In both the places where the Ten Commandments of Sinai are recited (Exodus 20:8–11 and Deuteronomy 5:12–15), it is made clear that the whole family, all servants, and "the foreigner within your gates" are all to rest one day of every seven. In the second recitation, the Bible explicitly says that the reason for this Sabbath rest is to remember what it was like to be a slave in Mitzraiim (the Hebrew word for Egypt means, more generally, "the tight and narrow place"), where it was never possible to rest.

Yet America today sneers at immigrants; blames the poor for their poverty; keeps at least 5 percent of its people officially unemployed, and in fact far more (prisoners and those who have given up on ever finding a job, for example); dumps many, many more from jobs long held into jobs far beneath their abilities for the sake of "efficient" management; subjects others to exhausting overwork that leaves no time for rest, reflection, celebration, family, love, community—and drives them to alcohol or television to relax. In that America—this America—what is the obligation of those who, like Boaz, are well-off?

Because Ruth and Boaz, the outcast and the solid citizen, got together, they could bring Messiah into the world—the transformation that brings peace and justice. What does that teach us today?

It teaches us to make sure that every human being can find decent work and be decently paid for it. To make sure that every human being has time for calm and reflective rest, time to live in the midst of a loving family and community. Only through a rhythm of worthy work and reflective rest do human beings grow into moral and ethical people.

For individuals to be ethically responsible, their society as a whole must be ethically responsible. We create an irresponsible society if we tell individuals they are responsible for themselves—and then deny them the jobs, the decent incomes, and the time for rest and renewal that we all need in order to be responsible human beings.

No one offered Ruth a pile of food, free for the taking. She was both entitled and obligated to glean the food, even though she did not own the land on which it grew. That was responsibility.

Restful renewal is also an aspect of responsibility. Ruth, like every other citizen or foreigner, like every worker, even the earth itself and all its life forms, was entitled and obligated to rest on the Sabbath. Time to repose and reflect, time for family, community, and citizenship.

But today we keep millions of our people unemployed, and force others to be overworked. For millions, no gleaning. For millions, no Sabbath.

Arthur Waskow, "Holy Economics," *Sojourners* (September/October 1997), www.sojo.net

# CHAPTER THREE

ג:א וַתֹּאמֶר לָהּ נָעֳמִי חֲמוֹתָהּ בִּתִּי הֲלֹא אֲבַקֶּשׁ־לָךְ מָנוֹחַ אֲשֶׁר
יִיטַב־לָךְ:

**3:1 NAOMI, HER MOTHER-IN-LAW, SAID TO HER, "DAUGHTER, I MUST FIND YOU A PLACE TO SETTLE, WHICH WILL BE GOOD FOR YOU.**

Naomi, the unsung hero of this book, seems less concerned with her own well-being than Ruth's. The reader can anticipate that the focus of this chapter will be on Ruth finding a place to settle down and call home. Naomi's language clearly indicates that she has fully accepted Ruth, as should the Jewish community into which she has brought Ruth.

This is a challenging verse to translate, because it is difficult to find the idiom that properly expresses the meaning behind the word *manoach* (ease, resting place). Ibn Ezra suggests that only a married woman can find *manoach*. If this is the case, then perhaps the word should be translated as "home." However, as the larger context implies, more than a "home" is required. A true change of status is desired. Naomi wants Ruth to have an easier time than she has had up to this moment, and Naomi believes that she will gain such ease by finding a life partner with whom she can make a "home." In the *Targum*, Naomi takes an oath that she will not rest until she finds such a place for Ruth.

ג:ב וְעַתָּה הֲלֹא בֹעַז מֹדַעְתָּנוּ אֲשֶׁר הָיִית אֶת־נַעֲרוֹתָיו הִנֵּה־הוּא זֹרֶה
אֶת־גֹּרֶן הַשְּׂעֹרִים הַלָּיְלָה:

**3:2 "NOW, NOTE THIS: BOAZ, OUR RELATIVE, THE ONE WITH WHOSE YOUNG FEMALE FIELD HANDS YOU WORKED, WILL BE WINNOWING BARLEY ON THE THRESHING FLOOR TONIGHT.**

Naomi is not satisfied with allowing things to transpire on their own. She wants to do what she can to ensure Ruth's happiness and security, so she offers Ruth specific advice and careful guidance. Naomi's naming of Boaz as "*our* relative" once again indicates that she has taken Ruth, formerly a Moabite, fully into her family. There is a bit of irony in the verse. While her reference to the female fieldworkers recalls Ruth's modesty in not working with men, Naomi will actually be encouraging Ruth to boldly approach and seduce Boaz.

Since the *Targum* has added "in the field" to the phrase "whose young women," we have rendered it as "young female field hands," to distinguish these workers from the young men who also worked in the field. The *Targum* also adds "in the wind of" to the word "tonight," amplifying the romantic implications in Naomi's statement. According to Rashi, since the period in which they lived was marked by thievery, Boaz was forced to spend the nights in the field during the harvest so that no one would steal his grain.

ג:ג וְרָחַצְתְּ וָסַכְתְּ וְשַׂמְתְּ שמלתך שִׂמְלֹתַיִךְ עָלַיִךְ ויředתי וְיָרַדְתְּ הַגֹּרֶן אַל־תִּוָּדְעִי לָאִישׁ עַד כַּלֹּתוֹ לֶאֱכֹל וְלִשְׁתּוֹת:

**3:3** "Wash yourself, put on perfume, put on your best dress, and go down to the threshing floor. But wait until he has finished eating and drinking before you let him know you are there.

These words are a mother-in-law's lessons on seduction to her daughter-in-law. While it seems like a strange posture for a mother-in-law to assume, the instructions are clear, as are the intended end results even though they are just hinted at. But because Naomi doesn't fully know Boaz's temperament, she wants to make sure that he is satiated before encouraging Ruth to approach him. What seems strange is that Ruth, a previously married woman, would need such advice.

In order to emphasize the obviously sexual nuances in Naomi's advice, the author uses a double entendre in the phrase *al tivadi la-ish* (literally, "don't make yourself known to the man"). The root *y-d-a* (know) can mean "have sexual intercourse," as it does in Genesis 4:1. Naomi is telling Ruth not to rush the situation.

We have followed the *Targum*, which adds *bosemin* (spices, or perfume) to the translation of *vasacht* (anoint yourself). The *Targum* also adds *utashavi tachshitin* (put on jewels [or jewelry]), a rather inconsistent comment for a women who is so poor that she has to glean the field for food. However, the point is simple: Naomi is suggesting that Ruth dress and adorn herself seductively.

Since Rashi translates *simlotayich* (your garments) as "your Sabbath clothing," we have translated it as "your best dress." He also gives a different reason for "washing": "to remove the traces of idolatry" and "to anoint" herself with "mitzvot," since she is a Moabite woman. Ibn Ezra, like the *Targum*, understands *vasacht* to mean "put on perfume" and "garments" as "the best you have."

ג:ד וִיהִי בְשָׁכְבוֹ וְיָדַעַתְּ אֶת־הַמָּקוֹם אֲשֶׁר יִשְׁכַּב־שָׁם וּבָאת וְגִלִּית

מַרְגְּלֹתָיו ושכבתי וְשָׁכָבְתְּ וְהוּא יַגִּיד לָךְ אֵת אֲשֶׁר תַּעֲשִׂין:

**3:4** "WHEN HE LIES DOWN, NOTE THE PLACE! WHILE HE IS
LYING THERE, GO OVER. UNCOVER HIS FEET AND LIE
DOWN. HE WILL TELL YOU WHAT TO DO."

The advice continues and it becomes clear to the reader what Naomi is sending Ruth
to do. But Naomi stops short. Instead she indicates that Boaz will tell Ruth what to
do. This suggests that either Naomi is telling Ruth that it is improper for women to
make overt sexual advances or that Boaz will indicate whether Ruth is welcome in
his bed.

There is a series of sexual double entendres in this verse. The root *sh-ch-v,* meaning
"to lie down," is used elsewhere to indicate sexual intercourse (e.g., Genesis 19:32,
19:35). The root *b-o-a* (with the last letter silent) means to "come" (translated here as
in the American English to "go over") and have sexual intercourse (e.g., Genesis 16:2,
30:3). The root *g-l-h* means to "uncover" and expose genitalia (e.g., Leviticus 20:11;
II Samuel 6:20). While *marg'lotav* means "[a place for] his feet," feet are often used
in the Bible as a euphemism for genitalia (e.g., Exodus 4:25; Isaiah 6:2, 7:20). The
verse strongly hints at what exactly Boaz will tell Ruth to do.

Rather more innocently, the *Targum* suggests that Ruth will ask for *ayta* (advice) and
Boaz *b'chochmatay* (in his wisdom) will tell Ruth what to do. Ibn Ezra avoids the
sexuality of the verse and simply explains "his [Boaz's] feet" on the basis on Daniel
10:6, more like his knees than his feet.

ג:ה וַתֹּאמֶר אֵלֶיהָ כֹּל אֲשֶׁר־תֹּאמְרִי [אֵלַי] אֶעֱשֶׂה:

**3:5** SHE ANSWERED, "WHATEVER YOU SAY, I WILL DO!"

Because of the straightforward nature of the verse, none of the commentators
consulted for this volume have anything to say about the verse. While this verse might
appear to be unnecessary—since the following verse tells us that Ruth does as she is
told—this verse indicates that Ruth agrees unconditionally to follow the instructions of
her mother-in-law. We have added the exclamation point at the end of the verse to
reflect such a sentiment.

ג:ו וַתֵּרֶד הַגֹּרֶן וַתַּעַשׂ כְּכֹל אֲשֶׁר־צִוַּתָּה חֲמוֹתָהּ:

**3:6** SHE WENT DOWN TO THE THRESHING FLOOR AND DID EVERYTHING THAT HER MOTHER-IN-LAW TOLD HER TO DO.

Ruth does not protest. She dutifully follows Naomi's directions. Rashi suggests that the word order of the verse implies that Ruth first goes to the threshing floor, then washes, perfumes, and adorns herself—allowing an onlooker to think that she is a prostitute. Ibn Ezra helps us to understand that the uncommon form *tzivatah* means ''commanded her.''

ג:ז וַיֹּאכַל בֹּעַז וַיֵּשְׁתְּ וַיִּיטַב לִבּוֹ וַיָּבֹא לִשְׁכַּב בִּקְצֵה הָעֲרֵמָה וַתָּבֹא בַלָּט וַתְּגַל מַרְגְּלֹתָיו וַתִּשְׁכָּב:

**3:7** BOAZ ATE, DRANK, AND WAS FEELING GOOD. HE WENT TO LIE DOWN NEXT TO A PILE OF GRAIN. SECRETLY, SHE CAME AND UNCOVERED HIS FEET, AND THEN SHE LAY DOWN.

The author paints a picture of Boaz that suggests that—after good food and drink—he is ready for Ruth's advances. Nevertheless, to emphasize that Boaz was not complicit, the author tells the reader that Ruth ''secretly'' approached Boaz and ''uncovered his feet.'' This latter phrase is a common biblical euphemism generally understood to mean uncovering or exposing nakedness. Essentially, Ruth exposes Boaz and then joins him, hardly a passive, modest act. The plain meaning of this text is quite explicit in its description of Ruth's behavior.

The commentators, however, are always concerned about biblical characters displaying normative behaviors. Since the *Targum* is troubled by Boaz's impropriety, exemplified by drinking too much and needing to lie down, it explains instead that he ''was feeling good'' because ''he praised the name of *Adonai*, who has removed famine from the Land of Israel.'' Rashi interprets ''feeling good'' as a result of Torah study. We have followed the *Targum* in its translation of *balat* as ''surreptitiously, quietly, secretly,'' although Rashi explains it as *b'nachat*, ''with ease, comfortably.''

ג:ח וַיְהִי בַּחֲצִי הַלַּיְלָה וַיֶּחֱרַד הָאִישׁ וַיִּלָּפֵת וְהִנֵּה אִשָּׁה שֹׁכֶבֶת מַרְגְּלֹתָיו:

### 3:8 AT ABOUT MIDNIGHT, THE MAN STIRRED AND TURNED, AND THERE WAS A WOMAN IN HIS BED!

The situation is clear. Boaz is sound asleep, perhaps a result of the drink referred to in verse 7. He does not even hear or feel Ruth when she enters his bed. Given the attention that Boaz gave to Ruth earlier, it is surprising that he is completely oblivious and, as we see in verse 9, seems not to have any idea who she is. Yet she may look different from the way she appeared working in the field. Perhaps she is simply unexpected.

The pivotal word in this verse is *vayilafeit*. The root *l-f-t* in its simplest form (what Hebrew linguists call *kal*) means "grasp, take hold of," as in Judges 16:29. The verb is found in another form (called *nifal*) in Job 6:18, where it means "twist around." The verb is constructed in the latter form in Ruth, but its meaning in this context is not clear. A similar Aramaic word, *lefet* (turnip), allowed the Rabbis of the Talmud (*Sanhedrin* 19b) and the otherwise usually decorous writer of the *Targum* to suggest that Boaz awakens with an erection. Surprised to find a woman in his bed, he loses it.

The *Targum* embellishes the verse, creating an entire scenario based on other biblical passages: "In the middle of the night, the man became frightened. He trembled and his flesh became as soft as a [cooked] turnip as a result. Then he saw the woman sleeping at his feet. He conquered his passion and did not approach her, in the same way that Joseph the Righteous refused to come near the Egyptian woman who was his master's wife (Genesis 39:7ff.) and Paltiel the Pious (I Samuel 25:44; II Samuel 3:15) stuck a sword [in the bed] between Michal, Saul's daughter and David's wife, and himself, so that he was unable to come close to her." While the *Targum* gives Boaz a great deal of credit for his virtue, it could also be viewed as a function of his temporary impotence.

Rashi explains the verse differently: Boaz trembled, because he thought a demon was in bed with him. When Boaz tried to scream, Ruth grabbed (literally, "grasped") him and embraced him with her arms. According to Rashi, Boaz realized that Ruth was a woman by touching her hair.

Ibn Ezra takes *vayilafeit* to mean "turn" and uses the verb from Job (6:18) to prove it. Rather than explaining it as "to touch," he argues that it actually means "to move side to side."

ג:ט וַיֹּאמֶר מִי־אָתְּ וַתֹּאמֶר אָנֹכִי רוּת אֲמָתֶךָ וּפָרַשְׂתָּ כְנָפֶךָ עַל־אֲמָתְךָ
כִּי גֹאֵל אָתָּה:

**3:9** HE SAID, "WHO ARE YOU?" SHE RESPONDED, "IT'S ME,
RUTH, YOUR MAIDSERVANT. SPREAD YOUR SKIRT OVER
YOUR MAIDSERVANT, FOR YOU ARE THE REDEEMING
RELATIVE."

If Boaz spreads his garment over Ruth, there will be no cloth separating them. Ruth's
words explicitly connect the possibility of sexual activity to Boaz's responsibility to
redeem her. There is also a sense from the text itself that it would not be proper for
Boaz to engage in a sexual act with Ruth without his willingness to take responsibility
for her afterward through serving as Ruth and Naomi's redeemer and making Ruth
his wife.

Though the sequence of events seems to be rapid, these events are the unfolding
of Naomi's carefully constructed plan. Ruth, a newcomer to the laws of levirate
marriage, has been guided by Naomi to persuade Boaz to accept his responsibility as
their redeemer. The human dimension in this verse is notable. It is easy to imagine
that unlike ourselves, biblical characters always did what the law required. However,
it is obvious from this text that even well-intentioned individuals sometimes had to
be encouraged to do what was proper, even through means the propriety of which
is questionable.

On the basis of Ezekiel 16:8, Koehler-Baumgartner (p. 486) takes the phrase
"spread your skirt over" to mean "to take someone as a spouse (literally, wife)." Note
that it is Ruth who initiates the action. The *Targum* strives to make it clear that Ruth
acted for the sake of marriage. It understands Ruth saying to Boaz, "Let your
maidservant take your name. Marry me to be your spouse, because you are the
redeemer."

Rashi explains *kanaf* (literally, "wing") as the edge of a garment, that is, that Boaz
covers Ruth with his *tallit*. He also interprets "spreading the garment" as a metaphor
for marriage. Rashi refers readers of the text to Leviticus 25:25, where the notion of
a relative as redeemer is explained. In a rather self-effacing manner that is typical
of the time in which Ruth was written, Ruth tells Boaz to redeem the property and
to take her as part of the property in order to preserve the name of her deceased
husband.

Ibn Ezra also explains the phrase to mean marriage but adds that Naomi told Ruth
that Jewish law required Boaz as the *go-eil* (redeemer) to marry her. He had no real
choice in the matter.

ג:י וַיֹּאמֶר בְּרוּכָה אַתְּ לַיהֹוָה בִּתִּי הֵיטַבְתְּ חַסְדֵּךְ הָאַחֲרוֹן מִן־
הָרִאשׁוֹן לְבִלְתִּי־לֶכֶת אַחֲרֵי הַבַּחוּרִים אִם־דַּל וְאִם־עָשִׁיר:

**3:10** HE SAID, "YOUNG WOMAN, MAY YOU BE BLESSED BY
*ADONAI*. YOUR LAST ACT OF KINDNESS IS BETTER
THAN THE FIRST INASMUCH AS YOU HAVE NOT
TURNED TO YOUNG MEN, POOR OR RICH.

Boaz remains surprised by Ruth's actions. He admits that he thought that a young, beautiful woman such as Ruth would turn her affections to a younger man. Here the author emphasizes the fact that Ruth takes seriously her new commitment to the Jewish people and is carefully following its rules regarding levirate marriage and redemption. Boaz's statement is further cause to celebrate Ruth's entry into the Jewish community.

The *Targum* identifies Ruth's first act of kindness as becoming a convert to Judaism. Her last act of kindness is related to the notion of levirate marriage. Ruth acted as if, committed to such a marriage with a boy, she had to wait until he grew old enough to marry her. In the interim, she had to remain chaste and not get involved with other young men, whether rich or poor.

Other commentators read this verse in different ways. Rashi understands Ruth's first act of kindness as a reference to Ruth's treatment of Naomi, while Ibn Ezra relates it to her conduct vis-à-vis her deceased husband. The words "poor or rich" indicate to Ibn Ezra that everyone loved Ruth because of her beauty.

ג:יא וְעַתָּה בִּתִּי אַל־תִּירְאִי כֹּל אֲשֶׁר־תֹּאמְרִי אֶעֱשֶׂה־לָּךְ כִּי יוֹדֵעַ
כָּל־שַׁעַר עַמִּי כִּי אֵשֶׁת חַיִל אָתְּ:

**3:11** "NOW, YOUNG WOMAN, DON'T BE AFRAID. WHATEVER
YOU SAY, I WILL DO FOR YOU. EVERYONE KNOWS THAT
YOU ARE A MARVELOUS WOMAN.

The word "knows" contains an idiom within an idiom. The verb has as its subject the phrase *kol shaar ami*, literally, "the entire gate of my people." The "gate" refers to the people who gather at the gate of the city (cf. Koehler-Baumgartner, p. 1616). These are the important people, the kind one would quote when saying "everyone knows," that is, "anyone who is anyone." We have translated *eishet chayil* (usually translated as a "woman of virtue," as in Proverbs 31:10) as a "marvelous woman." Nevertheless, the implication is that while one might suggest that Ruth's activity—to come into a man's bed prior to marriage—is not virtuous, Ruth is indeed a virtuous woman. This act will not spoil her reputation in the community.

The *Targum* explains the phrase "the entire gate of my people" as "all who sit in the gate of the Great Sanhedrin." In this reading, the words *eishet chayil* are meant to be understood as "you are a righteous woman and you have the strength to bear the yoke of the mitzvot of *Adonai*." While Rashi does not comment on the verse, Ibn Ezra refers his readers to his comment on Proverbs 31, where he suggests that such a woman attracts and acquires men through her wisdom.

ג:יב וְעַתָּה כִּי אָמְנָם כִּי אם גֹאֵל אָנֹכִי וְגַם יֵשׁ גֹאֵל קָרוֹב מִמֶּנִּי:

**3:12** "Now, although I am your relative bound to redeem [you], there is a nearer redeemer than me.

If Boaz is Ruth's closest relative, then he has the responsibility to redeem her. At this point, it is unclear who would be the more responsible party. Now that Boaz has made a commitment to Ruth, the author has to figure out how to skip over the other relative, who would have primary responsibility to her. Such effort on her behalf is also further proof of how quickly Ruth's status in the community has been accepted.

The *Targum* understands Boaz to say, "Truthfully, I am your redeemer. However, there is a more fitting redeemer than me." Rashi notes that the other *go-eil* (redeemer) has a more certain claim, though it is not clear why. He then refers readers to a rabbinic dispute (*Ruth Rabbah* 6:3; Babylonian Talmud, *Bava Batra* 91a) that discusses whether Boaz, Elimelech, and another man named Tov (see comment on 3:13) were brothers, or whether Elimelech, Tov, and another named Salmon were brothers. The eldest brother would have primary responsibility to Ruth. It is important to note the name Tov (good) is indicated as Elimelech's brother, as if to suggest he should do the good (right) thing with regard to Naomi and Ruth. We know very little about either Tov or Salmon except that Salmon is possibly Boaz's father. The dispute is resolved through the suggestion that "brother" can also refer to an "uncle." In either case, Tov was the relative nearest to Ruth. Thus, the midrash has Boaz say, "Tov is a brother, while I am the son of a brother."

ג:יג לִינִי הַלַּיְלָה וְהָיָה בַבֹּקֶר אִם־יִגְאָלֵךְ טוֹב יִגְאָל וְאִם־לֹא יַחְפֹּץ לְגָאֳלֵךְ וּגְאַלְתִּיךְ אָנֹכִי חַי־יְהוָה שִׁכְבִי עַד־הַבֹּקֶר:

**3:13** "Stay the night. When morning comes, if he will redeem you, [that's] good. If he won't redeem you, then, as *Adonai* lives, I will lie here until morning."

If we follow the Rabbis' view as expressed in the midrash and Talmud (*Ruth Rabbah* 6:5; Babylonian Talmud, *Bava Batra* 91a) that *tov* (literally, "good")—which we have

50

translated as "that's good"—is a proper name, then the verse should be translated as "if Tov will redeem you, let him" rather than as "if he will redeem you, [that's] great. Let him." However, neither the *Targum* nor any of the classic commentators take *tov* as a proper noun. In any case, Boaz wants Ruth to spend the night with him, promising her that either he or another relative will redeem her. He wants to allay any fears that the promise is made just to gain sexual favor.

In its translation, the *Targum* adds a few words to the verse. To "he," it adds, "the one who will redeem you by the Torah." To "I will," it adds, "I swear to God that whatever you have said, I will do." The *Targum* posits Boaz's behavior as following the rules set down in the Torah. Then it attempts to add a religious dimension to Boaz's words and raise them above a mere sexual encounter. The *Targum* also takes Boaz's reference to God and turns his words into an oath that obligates Boaz.

Rashi reads this verse as a dialogue between Boaz and Ruth. To Ruth, Boaz says, "'Stay the night' even without a man." She responds, "You are trying to seduce me with words." Boaz replies, "I swear that I am not trying to seduce you with words." Rashi adds that the Rabbis claimed that Boaz took an oath against the *yetzer hara* (the inclination to evil). The *yetzer hara* said to Boaz, "She is not married and you're not married. Have sex with her." Boaz responded that he will only have sex after he marries Ruth. Rashi's dialogue serves to support the image of Boaz as a good, righteous man.

Ibn Ezra raises doubts that *tov* was the name of the other relative who might redeem Ruth, since Boaz will address that person in the next chapter (4:1) as *p'loni almoni*, a common idiom that means "so-and-so" (see Koehler-Baumgartner, p. 934).

ג:יד וַתִּשְׁכַּב מרגלתו מַרְגְּלוֹתָיו עַד־הַבֹּקֶר וַתָּקָם בטרום בְּטֶרֶם יַכִּיר אִישׁ
אֶת־רֵעֵהוּ וַיֹּאמֶר אַל־יִוָּדַע כִּי־בָאָה הָאִשָּׁה הַגֹּרֶן:

**3:14** SO SHE LAY AT HIS FEET UNTIL DAYBREAK BUT GOT UP BEFORE [THERE WAS ENOUGH LIGHT FOR] ANYONE TO RECOGNIZE ANYONE ELSE, FOR HE HAD SAID, "DON'T LET ANYONE KNOW THAT A WOMAN CAME TO THE THRESHING FLOOR."

Boaz wants to protect Ruth's reputation in the community, especially if he is going to marry her. Also, he may recognize the fact that people often associate unchaste behavior with women who come from outside the Jewish community.

The *Targum*, which has set Boaz up as a righteous individual and Ruth as a virtuous woman, is eager to explain why "anyone [could not] recognize anyone else"—because of the darkness (*kodam chashocha*). The *Targum* also changes the person to whom Boaz directs his comments from Ruth to Boaz's servants. The change accomplishes one or both of two things. First, by telling his servants, Boaz is preempting any malicious rumor that they might be inclined to start. Second, if they were present, it meant that Boaz and Ruth were not alone and thus did not violate any prohibition concerning unmarried men and women alone together. Rashi, on the other hand, thinks that Boaz's statement is directed to Ruth. He reminds the reader that "[she] got up before...anyone [could] recognize anyone else." Rashi recognizes, as does the contemporary reader, that these are two complicit, consenting adults. Nevertheless, they are cautious not to violate any societal norms.

ג:טו וַיֹּאמֶר הָבִי הַמִּטְפַּחַת אֲשֶׁר־עָלַיִךְ וְאֶחֳזִי־בָה וַתֹּאחֶז בָּה וַיָּמָד

שֵׁשׁ־שְׂעֹרִים וַיָּשֶׁת עָלֶיהָ וַיָּבֹא הָעִיר:

**3:15** HE SAID, "TAKE THE SHAWL YOU'VE GOT ON AND HOLD IT OUT." SO SHE HELD OUT THE SHAWL. AND HE MEASURED OUT SOME BARLEY INTO IT. HE GAVE IT TO HER TO CARRY, AND [THEN] HE WENT BACK TO THE CITY.

Boaz's action is rather provocative. We know from 2:17 that she brought home a large amount of grain less than a day before. The action might be an indication that Boaz will always provide for Ruth, even though it appears as if Boaz is compensating Ruth for their night together. He might have provided her with grain so that if she is recognized, at least there is evidence as to why she was on the threshing floor. Although it seems like the author wants us to understand that normally women did not go there, it was less of an impropriety than if people were to learn that she and Boaz spent the night together.

As *Biblia Hebraica* (p. 1199) notes, a number of variant manuscripts read *vatavo* (and *she* came and went back to the city), while our text reads *vayavo* (and *he* came and went back). We have adopted the Masoretic reading, because *vatavo* (and *she* came) is found in the first words of the next verse. In addition, the *Targum* translates the last two words of the verse as *v'al Boaz l'karta* (and Boaz entered the city). Moreover, it would make sense for Boaz to leave the threshing floor as soon as Ruth left. Rashi comes to the same conclusion.

The *Targum* finds much more than barley in what Boaz gave Ruth. First, divine assistance for Ruth was contained in the barley. How else could she carry the weight of so much barley? Second, it contained a messianic prophecy that suggested that six people (David; Daniel; Daniel's three associates: Hananiah/Shadrach, Mishael/Meshach, and Azariah/Abed-nego; and the Messiah king) would descend from her. Finally, she learned that these six would be blessed with six different kinds of blessings.

As to why Boaz went back to the city, Rashi suggests that it would be embarrassing for him were it to become known that a woman came to him on the threshing floor, and so he left in a hurry.

ג:טז וַתָּבוֹא אֶל־חֲמוֹתָה וַתֹּאמֶר מִי־אַתְּ בִּתִּי וַתַּגֶּד־לָה אֵת כָּל־אֲשֶׁר
עָשָׂה־לָה הָאִישׁ:

3:16 RUTH CAME BACK TO HER MOTHER-IN-LAW, WHO SAID,
"WHO ARE YOU, MY DAUGHTER?" THEN SHE TOLD HER
ALL THAT THE MAN HAD DONE FOR HER.

While it seems strange that Naomi doesn't recognize Ruth, the author has already told us (3:14) that it was still dark outside. It might appear that Naomi is taken aback by Ruth's behavior—after all, she spent the night with Boaz—but Ruth was merely following Naomi's instructions. Naomi is really saying, "What happened to you? I don't recognize you." Ruth's encounter with Boaz has transformed her in some way, and Naomi recognizes that a change has taken place. Perhaps she has fallen in love again, or perhaps her changed expression is the relief of having found someone who will provide for and protect them. Naomi's surprise quickly abates as Ruth relates to Naomi her tryst with Boaz. The *Targum* adds the words *b'kritzta* (at daybreak) to explain the reasoning behind Naomi's question.

Ibn Ezra also is bothered by Naomi's question. He maintains that Naomi asked the question before she opened the door for Ruth to enter the house. He also quotes the view of Jonah the Grammarian, who suggested that Naomi used the phrase *mi at* (who are you?) to mean *mah hayah lach* (what happened to you?).

ג:יז וַתֹּאמֶר שֵׁשׁ־הַשְּׂעֹרִים הָאֵלֶּה נָתַן לִי כִּי אָמַר [אֵלַי] אַל־תָּבוֹאִי
רֵיקָם אֶל־חֲמוֹתֵךְ:

3:17 SHE SAID, "BECAUSE HE TOLD ME, 'DON'T GO HOME
TO YOUR MOTHER-IN-LAW EMPTY-HANDED,' HE GAVE
ME THESE SIX MEASURES OF BARLEY."

Since "six measures of barley" does not seem to be sufficient elucidation of "all that the man had done" for Ruth in verse 3:16, much of what transpired is left for the reader to speculate. With the exception of the promise of redemption—a significant act once realized—all Ruth reports on is an additional amount of grain.

We have added the term "measures" in our translation although it is missing in the Hebrew text. The *Targum* does the same thing in its addition of the word *s'in* (measures). Rashi derives a lesson from this missing word. He contends that it would have been impossible for Ruth to carry six measures. Thus, she must have carried six grains of barley. This would be a scriptural hint that Ruth would bear a son who would be blessed six times: with wisdom, understanding, counsel, strength, knowledge, and fear of God. If Rashi is correct about the amount of barely being too much to carry, it is hard to imagine that Ruth left the threshing floor unnoticed (v. 14).

ג:יח וַתֹּאמֶר שְׁבִי בִתִּי עַד אֲשֶׁר תֵּדְעִין אֵיךְ יִפֹּל דָּבָר כִּי לֹא יִשְׁקֹט הָאִישׁ כִּי־אִם־כִּלָּה הַדָּבָר הַיּוֹם:

**3:18** Naomi said, "My daughter, stay here until you know how things will turn out, for this man will not rest until he settles the matter today."

Naomi presents Ruth with romantic advice: "Don't make it so easy for him. Let's see what he is really prepared to do." The implication is that Ruth once again follows the advice of Naomi. Some may see this as manipulative on Naomi's part—and to a more limited extent on the part of Ruth, as well. Nevertheless, the author makes the reader quite aware of Naomi's strategic skills.

Naomi advises Ruth to stay put so that Boaz can finish what he started—transforming a one-night-stand sexual relationship into the commitment of marriage. The *Targum* specifies rather that Ruth should stay *b'vaytai* (in the house). It also tells us that things will turn out from heaven, where "it is decreed and the Word is explained." Finally, the *Targum* explains that Boaz will "settle...the matter today" means that "he will work for good today." Rashi adds *ha-ish* (the man) to "he settles the matter today." Ibn Ezra notes that since all decrees come from heaven, the verb *yipol* (will fall) is used, rather than another verb to indicate the origin and direction of the action.

## *Levirate Marriage*

In Hebrew *yibum*, levirate marriage, refers to the responsibility of a man to marry his deceased brother's childless widow in order to raise children in the name of the deceased and carry on his name. If the surviving brother does not want to marry his sister-in-law, he must perform a ritual called *chalitzah*, as described in Deuteronomy 25:5–10, so that she can marry someone else. While any brother may fulfill the requirement of levirate marriage, the responsibility usually fell to the oldest surviving brother. The prohibition of polygamy complicates matters, but provisions still exist for it in modern Israel. The Reform and Conservative movements disregard levirate marriage, although there is some theoretical discussion of it among Conservative scholars.

## Great Sanhedrin

The Great Sanhedrin, the primary Jewish court, whose name is derived from Greek, held primary authority in the Land of Israel during the Roman and Byzantine periods. According to Hellenistic sources, its leader was the High Priest. However, according to rabbinic sources, the Sanhedrin was an assembly of sages led by scholars (specifically, the *nasi*, or president, and the *av beit din*, head of the court). The court consisted of seventy-one members who met in the ancient Temple in Jerusalem in what was called the Chamber of the Hewn Stone. This court appointed smaller courts of twenty-three members who met in regions around the country. While most of the authority of the Great Sanhedrin had to do with religious issues, the court maintained some legislative and political functions. The Sanhedrin was abolished around 425 C.E. when the patriarchate was introduced.

## Yetzer Hara

The Rabbis have taught that every person is endowed with a *yetzer hatov* and a *yetzer hara*, loosely translated as an instinctive inclination to do good and an inclination to do evil. The creative tension between these two forces prods us forward in life. These concepts form the foundation of rabbinic psychology and anthropology. The *yetzer hara* is not intrinsically evil. Rather, it is raw, untamed energy that manifests itself in the form of drives, especially sexual. Nevertheless, without it, according to the Rabbis, one would not be driven to marry, have children, build a home, or engage in business (*B'reishit Rabbah* 9:7). Of course, the Rabbis teach that the most effective antidote is the study of Torah (Babylonian Talmud, *Kiddushin* 30b).

## Masoretic Text

Jewish scribes working from 500 to 1000 C.E. were known as the Masoretes. They meticulously copied the Scriptures and preserved them. While the original Hebrew had no vowels and only consonants, as the Torah scroll itself remains without vowels, the Masoretes set the vowels. The work of the Masoretes produced the Masoretic text of the Bible (i.e., the current Hebrew text). The translation in this volume is based on the text called Lenigrad Codex/Ben Asher, which is thought to provide the closest rendering of the original Masoretic text. The Masoretes also set the musical notes for reading the Bible known in Yiddish as *trope* and in Hebrew as *taamei hamikra*.

# *Jonah the Grammarian (ca. 996–1050)*

Rabbi Jonah was probably the greatest Hebrew grammarian and lexicographer of the Middle Ages. He was born in Cordova and studied in Lucena. He eventually settled in Saragossa, where he lived until his death. While he was trained as a physician, his interest seemed to lie more in the area of Hebrew language. He contended that rational biblical exegesis should be based on a scientific understanding of the Hebrew language. While he never composed an actual commentary on the Bible, his work influenced numerous other commentators, including Ibn Ezra.

# GLEANINGS

## *Marriage as a Reflection of World Order*

Over the course of Jewish history, the ways in which Jews have understood their relationship with God—their covenant—have changed dramatically. But at least until modern times, few Jews even attempted a theory of Jewish life that did not have covenant at its core; as a result, the customs and practices of traditional Judaism have always sought to provide both individual Jews and Jewish communities with concrete ways of expressing their relationship with God. One of the most significant insights of traditional Judaism has been its contention that a relationship cannot exist in a vacuum. Just as one could not successfully sustain a relationship of love with another human being without expressing that love in numerous observable ways, so too does the Jew's relationship with God require concrete expression. . . .

   This human relationship, fashioned in the shadow, or image, of one's relationship to God, would both further the classic Jewish goal of investing human life with sanctity and serve as a model of how Jews might think about their infinitely more subtle covenant with God. In Jewish thought, the relationship most approximating that between human beings and God is the marital relationship between a man and a woman. An exploration of the Jewish traditions surrounding weddings and married life will reveal not only the significance of the various elements of the rituals themselves, but also the fundamental religious and theological claims that lie "behind the scenes" of the Jewish conception of marriage.

Daniel Gordis, "Marriage: Judaism's 'Other' Covenantal Relationship,"
in *Celebration and Renewal: Rites of Passage in Judaism*, ed. Rela M. Monson
(Philadelphia: Jewish Publication Society of America, 1993), 90–91

## *The Body in Love*

We are taught to love virtues, values, and ways of thinking, but we find ourselves drawn to a smile, a touch, a voice. Judaism has given us the Song of Songs to guide us in confronting society's separation between spirituality and sex. You can learn, through the Song of Songs, to delight in your body because your beloved delights in it despite its imperfections. But the eroticism in the Song of Songs has a meaning beyond simple sexuality. Eros is the core longing of the self for connecting with others. It has been said that the door to the invisible must be visible. Similarly, the door to the abstract must be tangible. Love begins with the visible, the tangible, the embodied; Freud characterized the force of Eros as that which seeks to combine organic substances into ever larger unities.

Carol Ochs, *Our Lives as Torah: Finding God in Our Own Stories*
(San Francisco: Jossey-Bass, 2001), 124–25

## *Loneliness*

"The other reason I know there is a God is loneliness. It is loneliness that drives the *Midat ha-Din* [God's just side] to risk losing control, risk being absolute, and making itself vulnerable enough to connect to someone. It is loneliness that teaches the *Midat ha-Rahamin* [God's merciful side that gives balance to the *Midat ha-Din*] to let loved ones go, take risks, be free, in order to retain them. It is loneliness that teaches people that winning arguments isn't always finding happiness. It is loneliness that makes the growth and compromise necessary for relationship, family, and community.

"Loneliness proves that there is a soul. It is loneliness that takes us past being an animal. It is loneliness that teaches us that real hunger can never be satisfied by eating, or having, or owning, or dominating, but only by sharing. It is loneliness that teaches people delayed gratification—and spiritual truth and ethical living are all rooted in delay.

"It is the feeling of being alone that teaches us that we need not be alone. The steps involved in being with others in a permanent, on-going, satisfying way teach meaning, not gratification; commitment to struggle, not being right; the need for balance, not monolithic truth. Suddenly I knew that when I feel alone, I know that there is God. Loneliness is the 60-cycle hum of the human soul being plugged in, but not yet in motion."

. . . When Adam and Eve ate the fruit of the Tree of the Knowledge of Good and Evil, the Tree that was also in the middle of the Garden, the Tree of Life, the force that changed them, that told them that they were naked, that forever changed humanity, that was the retrovirus of loneliness. For it is loneliness that always motivates first the search and then the finding.

Joel Lurie Grishaver, *The Bonding of Isaac: Stories and Essays about Gender and Jewish Spirituality*
(Los Angeles: Alef Design Group, 1997), 15

57

## Jewish Woman as Siren

From a male "gaze," women existed primarily in the sexual arena. According to Jewish law, the male sexual urge had only one legitimate outlet: A man could not legally masturbate; homosexual contact was taboo; nocturnal emission was discouraged by frightening stories of Lilith, and other female sexual demons who used semen to create demon children (*Zohar* I 54b). Sexual desire was to be fulfilled only in the marital bed. In addition, marital sex was restricted to two weeks in the month due to the laws of menstrual "purity." Women thus served as the objects of a considerable amount of pent up, repressed, and sublimated male sexual need. Women were not just desirable; according to Rabbinic thought, we were the powerful source of the male sexual drive. Our hair, arms, voices, legs could, according to cultural belief, inspire even the holiest man to forget his spiritual quest and become a mere puppet in thrall to the nearest woman.

Each woman, just by virtue of being a woman, was the Siren, at least to her own husband. She didn't need to wear make-up or work out. She didn't have to go on diets and look like a fashion model; in fact, this Siren was supposed to wear concealing clothing and hide her hair in order to present a less compelling temptation to the poor men (other than her husband) who had to have contact with her. She was the most sexually powerful, alluring being on earth.

Jane Rachel Litman, "Sexuality and Ritual Purity: When the Siren Stops Singing," in *Lifecycles: Jewish Women on Biblical Themes in Contemporary Life,* vol. 2, ed. Debra Orenstein and Jane Rachel Litman (Woodstock, VT: Jewish Lights Publishing, 1997), 191

## Identity and Choice

The convert lives with a double standard. According to the Rabbis, a convert is every bit as Jewish as a born Jew (BT *Yevamot* 47b)—and yet...things are different. The born Jew may take no interest in his/her Jewishness, or even try to hide it. S/he may exist as a "negative" Jew. But this option makes no sense for a convert: If you had no interest in Judaism, nor any intention of living a positively-identified Jewish life, you would not become Jewish. Because your Jewishness comes by an intellectual and spiritual choice, and not by simply being born, you are compelled to an intense self-scrutiny. This self-consciousness parallels that of Jews throughout the millennia who were constantly reminded of their Jewishness in Christian and Muslim lands. Converts are thus different from other Jews and also, paradoxically, the most "Jewish" of the Jews.

By converting, you are not joining a club or culture or even an ideology—you are becoming a member of a people, taking on a new identity. You will begin to experience *history* differently, and to take part in it differently. If you read a book or see a film that deals with the Holocaust, for example, you will say "These are *my* people,'' and when you hear news of Israel on the radio, you might stop whatever you are doing and listen, for it is *your* news. You will experience your *present* differently. Your relationship with your family will change: No more helping Mom trim the tree or going with her to midnight Mass. These are just the obvious examples— there will be many subtle changes as well. You will have to explain yourself to family or friends, who may be mystified at why you are ''rejecting'' them by becoming Jewish, and you may be surprised at the odd notions new friends or neighbors harbor about you on account of your Jewishness. Your decision will affect the *future*, as well. By raising Jewish children, becoming involved in the Jewish social action projects, or simply bringing a Jewish perspective to whatever you do in the world, you will be woven into the great tapestry of Jewish destiny. That tapestry will look different on account of you.

Shoshana Brown, ''Dear Ruth: Letter to an Aspiring Convert,'' in *Lifecycles: Jewish Women on Life Passages and Personal Milestones,* vol. 1, ed. Debra Orenstein (Woodstock, VT: Jewish Lights Publishing, 1994), 236–37

# CHAPTER FOUR

וּבֹעַז עָלָה הַשַּׁעַר וַיֵּשֶׁב שָׁם וְהִנֵּה הַגֹּאֵל עֹבֵר אֲשֶׁר דִּבֶּר־בֹּעַז
וַיֹּאמֶר סוּרָה שְׁבָה־פֹּה פְּלֹנִי אַלְמֹנִי וַיָּסַר וַיֵּשֵׁב: ד:א

**4:1** NOW BOAZ WENT UP TO THE GATE AND TOOK HIS SEAT THERE. JUST THEN, THE REDEEMER OF WHOM BOAZ HAD SPOKEN PASSED BY. HE SAID TO HIM, "HEY FRIEND, COME OVER AND SIT HERE." SO THE PERSON CAME OVER AND SAT DOWN.

Boaz follows through on what he had promised Ruth. While it appears as if Boaz just happens upon the unnamed relative, he obviously knew where to find him. Nevertheless, while it is apparent that Boaz's place in society afforded him a seat at the city gate, it is unclear whether his relative had such a similar seat or was just walking through the area. If the latter is the case, then Boaz has the opportunity to exert influence over his relative. And if the relative was without means, he may not have felt that he was in a position to redeem Ruth irrespective of his responsibility to her. A measure of disdain is contained in the words Boaz uses to beckon his relative. But the relative responds without hesitation and sits as he is told.

The gate to the city—any city—was usually where its leaders sat, offered counsel, and issued judgments. Having a "seat" there was looked upon as an honor. The gate area was considered to be a place of power and influence. The *Targum* explains that the gate to which Boaz went was *bayt dinah d'sanhedrin* (the court of the Sanhedrin). It also explains *p'loni almoni* (literally, "so-and-so," which we have translated as "hey friend") as *g'var d'tzeean ohrchatay* (the one whose ways are hidden). The implication isn't just that his name was unknown, but also his motivation for agreeing not to marry Ruth.

Rashi explains that *p'loni almoni*'s name was not given because of his unwillingness to redeem Ruth. Perhaps the author did not want to honor his inaction by giving him a name (as in reputation). The author may also be refusing to name the relative as a literary device to heighten reader interest in the dramatic story. Rashi also notes that the *Targum* translates *p'loni almoni* in I Samuel 21:3 as *kasi v'tamir* (covered and hidden), consistent with its interpretation here. He derives *p'loni* from the root *p-l-a* (to be wondrous, marvelous) as in *ki yipalei mimcha* (if it be too marvelous) in Deuteronomy 17:8, meaning "is it too difficult?" Rashi cites a further example of the root in Genesis 18:14: *hayipalei mei-Adonai* (is it too marvelous for God?). He derives *almoni* from *alman* (widower). In other words, in Rashi's reading this unnamed person was separated from the words of the Torah. The person didn't want to marry Ruth because of her outsider status, but he should have known that the prohibition against the Ammonites and Moabites marrying into the Israelite community applied to Moabite men and not women. It is not hard to imagine that while Ruth may have been accepted by the Jewish community, there would still be many people who would see her as a "second-class citizen," since she was not born into the Jewish people.

ד:ב וַיִּקַּח עֲשָׂרָה אֲנָשִׁים מִזִּקְנֵי הָעִיר וַיֹּאמֶר שְׁבוּ־פֹה וַיֵּשֵׁבוּ:

**4:2** BOAZ TOOK TEN ELDERS OF THE TOWN AND SAID TO THEM, "TAKE A SEAT." SO THEY SAT DOWN.

From the speed with which the elders appear to respond and react to Boaz, it would seem that he is an influential individual. The motivation behind Boaz's request is clear—he has promised results, and he proceeds to get them. He is anxious to return to Ruth. The "elders" were those who governed the town or, at least, provided guidance to those who ruled. The reference to the number ten in this verse reinforces the notion that these elders represent the entire community. We have added Boaz's name to the beginning of the verse for the sake of clarity.

ד:ג וַיֹּאמֶר לַגֹּאֵל חֶלְקַת הַשָּׂדֶה אֲשֶׁר לְאָחִינוּ לֶאֱלִימֶלֶךְ מָכְרָה נָעֳמִי הַשָּׁבָה מִשְּׂדֵה מוֹאָב:

**4:3** HE SAID TO THE REDEEMER, "NAOMI—WHO HAS COME BACK FROM THE LAND OF MOAB—IS ABOUT TO SELL A SECTION OF A FIELD THAT BELONGED TO OUR RELATIVE ELIMELECH.

While Boaz directs his comment to the redeemer, the previously unidentified relative who has not come to Naomi and Ruth's aid, Boaz is obviously speaking to the elders as well. Both his posture and the context he sets up suggest the image of a prosecuting attorney making his opening statement in a courtroom.

While this verse appears rather straightforward, the word *machrah* (literally, "she sold") presents us with a challenge. If Naomi has already sold the piece of land, then what follows would be irrelevant. There would be no point in telling the redeemer about the transaction if it had already been completed and title to the land had already passed to a new owner. In order to meet this challenge, Koehler-Baumgartner (p. 581) proposes that we read the word as an irregular form of the participle *mochrah*. This would give the sense (as a participle often does) of an action that is about to occur. Thus, it would be taken as "desire[s] to sell." Therefore, we have translated it as "about to sell." The *Targum*, however, translates it in a straightforward manner as *zabnat* (she sold). The difficulty does not capture the attention of Rashi or Ibn Ezra. But Ibn Ezra does suggest that the phrase "section of the field" implies that the field was very large and Elimelech owned only a part of it.

ד:ד וַאֲנִי אָמַרְתִּי אֶגְלֶה אָזְנְךָ לֵאמֹר קְנֵה נֶגֶד הַיֹּשְׁבִים וְנֶגֶד זִקְנֵי עַמִּי אִם־תִּגְאַל גְּאָל וְאִם־לֹא יִגְאַל הַגִּידָה לִּי וְאֵדַע וְאֵדְעָה כִּי אֵין זוּלָתְךָ לִגְאוֹל וְאָנֹכִי אַחֲרֶיךָ וַיֹּאמֶר אָנֹכִי אֶגְאָל׃

**4:4** "I SAID TO MYSELF, I SHOULD TELL YOU WHAT HAPPENED AND SAY, 'TAKE TITLE WITH THESE MEN SEATED HERE AND THE ELDERS OF MY PEOPLE AS WITNESSES.' IF YOU ARE GOING TO REDEEM, DO SO! IF YOU ARE NOT GOING TO REDEEM, SAY SO! SINCE THERE IS NO ONE AHEAD OF YOU AND I COME AFTER YOU, I WILL, THEN, KNOW WHAT TO DO." HE REPLIED, "I WILL REDEEM."

Boaz is careful about doing what is right and making sure that his relative knows what is at stake. He also wants to assure the elders that he has not acted presumptuously, but that he will fulfill his obligation to Naomi and Ruth if his relative does not. Boaz also reminds him that the elders are able to affirm a transfer of property should he desire to do so. Boaz continues to give the man every opportunity to act responsibly.

The difficulty in translating Hebrew idioms into English idioms makes this verse particularly hard to understand. The first verb, *amarti* (I said) suggests a reflective conversation. Thus, we have translated it as "I said to myself." The next phrase, *egleh ozn'cha* (literally, "I will reveal to your ear"), is translated as "I should tell you." It is obvious from the context that the next phrase, *k'nei neged hayoshvim* (literally, "buy in the presence of those who sit"), has a specific judicial meaning. *K'nei* means more than just "buy." And the people described in the verse do more than just "sit." Therefore, we translated it as "Take title . . . as witnesses."

There is an additional difficulty the second time the word "redeem" is used. The Masoretic text has it as *lo yigal*, "he will not redeem." We would expect it to read *lo tigal*, "you will not redeem." Interestingly, the *Targum* does read *tigal*, as do numerous manuscripts, according to *Biblia Hebraica* (p. 1199). It is possible therefore that earlier biblical texts, no longer extant, in fact read *tigal*.

In its translation, the *Targum* specifies those seated as "those seated in the gate of the court of the Sanhedrin." It also explains that "the only one" refers to "the one who is permitted [to redeem]." Rashi explains "the only one" as the one who was a relative.

In his comment on the verse, Ibn Ezra focuses on the unusual grammar, using Malachi 2:15 ("Do not betray/*al yivgod* the wife of your youth") as an example in which the masculine form is used when we would expect the feminine form, although it has the same sense: Don't betray.

ד:ה וַיֹּאמֶר בֹּעַז בְּיוֹם־קְנוֹתְךָ הַשָּׂדֶה מִיַּד נָעֳמִי וּמֵאֵת רוּת הַמּוֹאֲבִיָּה אֵשֶׁת־הַמֵּת קָנִיתִי לְהָקִים שֵׁם־הַמֵּת עַל־נַחֲלָתוֹ:

4:5 BOAZ THEN SAID, "ON THE DAY THAT YOU TAKE TITLE TO THE FIELD FROM NAOMI, YOU WILL HAVE ALSO ACQUIRED RUTH THE MOABITE, THE SPOUSE OF THE DECEASED, TO ESTABLISH THE NAME OF THE DECEASED UPON HIS INHERITANCE."

The legal verses are confusing even after they are clearly translated and explained. As much as Boaz wants Ruth, he tells the relative that the redemption of the land and Ruth go together. At the same time, Boaz reminds the relative of the purpose of fulfilling his obligations to Ruth.

Understanding the verse is made difficult by the word *mei-eit* (from). As it is presented in the text, the acquisition of the field is to be accomplished *miyad Naomi* (from Naomi) *umei-eit Rut* (from Ruth). In 4:3, we read that it was "Naomi . . . [who] was about to sell" the field. No mention was made of Ruth. There was no indication that she had title of the property or that she was interested in selling it. As the verse stands, the last clause does not relate to the beginning of the verse. The *Biblia Hebraica* (p. 1199) brings the two sections of the verse together by suggesting a change for *mei-eit* to *gam et* (also). We have followed that suggestion in our translation.

The *Targum* takes the verse as it stands but clarifies it by adding "you have to redeem and are required to have a levirate marriage and to take her [Ruth] as a spouse in order to establish the name of the deceased upon his inheritance." Although Rashi does not emend the text, he takes *mei-eit* to indicate that the redeemer is obligated to buy the field but Ruth would be unwilling to sell it unless she marries the buyer/redeemer as well. Ibn Ezra suggests that the word *kanitah* (you have bought, you have acquired) should be understood as something that will take place in the future.

ד:ו וַיֹּאמֶר הַגֹּאֵל לֹא אוּכַל לִגְאָול לִגְאָל־לִי פֶּן־אַשְׁחִית אֶת־נַחֲלָתִי
גְּאַל־לְךָ אַתָּה אֶת־גְּאֻלָּתִי כִּי לֹא־אוּכַל לִגְאֹל:

**4:6** THE REDEEMER SAID, "I AM NOT ABLE TO REDEEM
BECAUSE I MIGHT DESTROY MY OWN INHERITANCE.
SINCE I AM NOT ABLE TO REDEEM, YOU SHOULD
DO SO."

The relative wants to make sure that Boaz and the elders understand that his inaction emerges from a sense of propriety and not irresponsibility. Then he quickly transfers the obligation to Boaz, making sure that Boaz knows that he will not protest at all when Boaz redeems Ruth.

The *Targum* expands on the verse, having the redeemer say, "In such a case, I am unable to redeem because I have a wife and I have no right to marry another [woman] in addition to her, which would cause contention in my home and would destroy my inheritance. Because you [Boaz] don't have a spouse, you should redeem [her] since I can't." Rashi understands "inheritance" as "seed, progeny." According to Rashi, the redeemer did not realize that the biblical prohibition regarding marrying Moabites applied to both men and women, but this was based on an incorrect understanding by the redeemer of Deuteronomy 23:4.

Ibn Ezra understands the word "inheritance" as a reference to the redeemer's property, although he notes that some thought that the word referred to the redeemer's wife. He reads "you should [do so]" as the redeemer giving permission to Boaz—who is next in line—to take appropriate action.

ד:ז וְזֹאת לְפָנִים בְּיִשְׂרָאֵל עַל־הַגְּאוּלָּה וְעַל־הַתְּמוּרָה לְקַיֵּם כָּל־דָּבָר
שָׁלַף אִישׁ נַעֲלוֹ וְנָתַן לְרֵעֵהוּ וְזֹאת הַתְּעוּדָה בְּיִשְׂרָאֵל:

**4:7** THIS USED TO BE THE PRACTICE IN ISRAEL: TO
ESTABLISH AN ACT OF REDEMPTION OR EXCHANGE,
ONE WOULD HAVE TO TAKE OFF ONE'S SANDAL AND
GIVE IT TO SOMEONE ELSE. THIS COUNTED AS
CORROBORATION IN ISRAEL.

The purpose of this verse seems to be to point out to the reader that the practice described in Ruth may be different from the one with which the reader may be familiar. Such a statement can only be made if the author is describing historical events rather than contemporaneous ones.

Although in Modern Hebrew *t'udah* means "certificate" or "document," we have followed Koehler-Baumgartner (p. 1768), which suggests that *v'zot hat'udah* should be translated as "this counted as corroboration." The modern *t'udah* functions to testify or corroborate what is stated in the document itself, such as citizenship in Israel.

The *Targum* changes "sandal" to *narta yad* (sleeve), specifying the "sleeve" as *yeminay* (the right one), and requires that the process be *kawdam saadayya* (before witnesses). Such a change suggests that an alternative practice was observed that used a sleeve rather than a sandal.

Rashi explains that the word *g'ulah* (redemption) refers to "selling" and the somewhat uncommon word *t'murah* (exchange) is a synonym for the more familiar word *chalifin* (exchanges, barter). He notes that taking off a sandal was the means to indicate the passing of title and the acquisition of ownership. In Rashi's time, pulling a sheet from hand to hand symbolized the passing of title from one person to another. He makes reference to the fact that there was a rabbinic controversy (Babylonian Talmud, *Bava M'tzia* 47a) regarding the precise procedure of who is to pass what to whom in this verse. Additionally, Rashi takes *v'zot hat'udah* as *mishpat ha-eidut* (a testimony used in court).

Ibn Ezra explains *l'fanim* (used to be) as "what happened in ancient days." He prefers the explanation of *hat'udah* as "testimony that is being sworn to" rather than the view of others who explain the term as "customary behavior."

ד:ח וַיֹּאמֶר הַגֹּאֵל לְבֹעַז קְנֵה־לָךְ וַיִּשְׁלֹף נַעֲלוֹ:

**4:8** WHEN THE REDEEMER SAID TO BOAZ, "YOU TAKE TITLE," HE TOOK OFF HIS SANDAL.

Since the redeemer transferred the responsibility of redemption to Boaz, Boaz is directed to remove his sandal. Once Boaz takes off his sandal, which he immediately does, Boaz is acknowledging his willingness to take on the act of redemption.

Consistent with the lack of clarity noted by the Rabbis in the previous verse, the text of this verse also does not make clear who it was who took off his sandal, Boaz or the redeemer. The *Targum* holds that it is Boaz who acted. However, as noted above, in the *Targum* he removed his right sleeve, not his sandal.

Ibn Ezra informs his readers that it was Boaz who removed his sandal and gave it to the redeemer. He notes, however, that there are those who believe that it was the reverse: the redeemer removed his sandal and gave it to Boaz.

Perhaps the author intentionally did not make the text clear in order to add to the suspense of the story. Since the relative had consistently refused to take on the responsibility, and seeing where the story leads, it seems likely that Boaz removed his own sandal. One might assume from Ibn Ezra's comments that Boaz gave his relative a sandal in order to give him but one more opportunity to act responsibly. However, it is more likely that Boaz presented the sandal to his relative as a way of "rubbing it in." If it is correct that the redeemer gave the shoe to Boaz, it seems unlikely that the story would continue as it does. Nevertheless, it could be argued that the redeemer humbly gave Boaz his shoe so that Boaz could use it in the transaction.

וַיֹּאמֶר בֹּעַז לַזְּקֵנִים וְכָל־הָעָם עֵדִים אַתֶּם הַיּוֹם כִּי קָנִיתִי אֶת־ ד:ט
כָּל־אֲשֶׁר לֶאֱלִימֶלֶךְ וְאֵת כָּל־אֲשֶׁר לְכִלְיוֹן וּמַחְלוֹן מִיַּד נָעֳמִי:

**4:9** Boaz made the following declaration to the elders and the rest of the people: "Today you are witnesses to my taking title from Naomi of everything that belonged to Elimelech, and everything that belonged to Chilion and Mahlon.

In order to echo the implicit quality of Boaz's statement, we have chosen to translate *vayomer Boaz* (literally, "and Boaz said") as "Boaz made the following declaration." The fact that the author introduces "the rest of the people" in this verse suggests that the exchange had become a public spectacle. There is perhaps even an implication that Boaz is playing to the audience somewhat. Implicit in taking title is the acceptance of all obligations relevant to the properties. While he relieves Naomi of any obligations, it is also clear that, as a woman, her entitlements were limited.

וְגַם אֶת־רוּת הַמֹּאֲבִיָּה אֵשֶׁת מַחְלוֹן קָנִיתִי לִי לְאִשָּׁה לְהָקִים ד:י
שֵׁם־הַמֵּת עַל־נַחֲלָתוֹ וְלֹא־יִכָּרֵת שֵׁם־הַמֵּת מֵעִם אֶחָיו וּמִשַּׁעַר
מְקוֹמוֹ עֵדִים אַתֶּם הַיּוֹם:

**4:10** "I take title as well to Mahlon's spouse, Ruth the Moabite. I, thereby, keep alive the name of the deceased over what he owned. That name will not disappear from his family nor from the place he came from. You are witnesses."

While Boaz separates the issues of taking title to property from taking on the responsibility for supporting Ruth, it is clear that she too is considered chattel. But his emphasis of her former status as a Moabite indicates that he meant to make it clear that he knows what he is doing—taking someone who was not born into the covenant as his wife. His status in the community also indicates that acting as a role model was an important public statement for encouraging the welcoming of newcomers into the Jewish community. Boaz also makes clear that his motivation is primarily altruistic—to ensure that the family name does not disappear. The author anticipates that children will be born from this union, which is the primary motivation behind the laws of levirate marriage.

Translating idioms is among the most challenging of tasks facing a translator. We have rendered *l'hakim shem hameit* (literally, "establish the name of the deceased") as "keep alive the name of the deceased." While "name" often refers to reputation, in this case it seems to refer specifically to the family name of the deceased. Similarly we have translated *v'lo yikareit* (literally, "shall not be cut off") as "shall not disappear." *Shaar m'komo* (literally, "the gate of his place") suggests the public space—the area surrounding the gate to the city—of his city of origin. For this reason we translated it as "the place he came from."

ד:יא וַיֹּאמְרוּ כָּל־הָעָם אֲשֶׁר־בַּשַּׁעַר וְהַזְּקֵנִים עֵדִים יִתֵּן יְהֹוָה אֶת־
הָאִשָּׁה הַבָּאָה אֶל־בֵּיתֶךָ כְּרָחֵל וּכְלֵאָה אֲשֶׁר בָּנוּ שְׁתֵּיהֶם
אֶת־בֵּית יִשְׂרָאֵל וַעֲשֵׂה־חַיִל בְּאֶפְרָתָה וּקְרָא־שֵׁם בְּבֵית לָחֶם:

**4:11** ALL THE PEOPLE AND THE ELDERS PRESENT AT THE GATE ANSWERED, "WE ARE WITNESSES. MAY GOD MAKE THIS WOMAN WHO ENTERS YOUR HOUSE BE AS RACHEL AND LEAH, WHO BOTH BUILT THE HOUSE OF ISRAEL. MAY YOU DO WELL IN EPHRATHAH AND GAIN FAME IN BETHLEHEM.

The statement of the elders makes Ruth's status clear. Though she is a Jew-by-choice, she is placed alongside the matriarchs Rachel and Leah. Let there be no doubt of the important role that converts to Judaism played—and continue to play—in Jewish history. This is a fulfillment of the declaration in 1:16–17. Ruth's actions, like those of Rachel and Leah, are important foundations for building the House of Israel.

The Koehler-Baumgartner *Lexicon* (p. 891) suggests that the phrase *vaaseih chayil* (literally, "to acquire wealth") refers to the acquiring of "power through a large family." We have simply translated it as "may you do well."

Emphasizing the legal aspect of the transaction, the *Targum* adds "of the Sanhedrin" after "the gate" and explains that "built the House of Israel" is a reference to the twelve tribes.

While Jewish tradition generally mentions Rachel before Leah, there has recently been a great deal of debate among liturgists in the Reform Movement concerning the order of listing these matriarchs. When the names of the Matriarchs were added to the *Avot* section of the *T'filah* in the gender-sensitive version of *Gates of Prayer*, the order used was "Leah and Rachel." In creating the new Reform siddur, *Mishkan T'filah,* the debate has centered around reversing this order back to the more traditional order found in other blessings and used in the egalitarian version of the Conservative *Siddur Sim Shalom* and the Reconstructionist *Kol Haneshamah*. Rashi notes that the order of Rachel and Leah (which is neither the birth order of the sisters nor the order of Jacob's marriage to them) indicates that even the children of Leah acknowledged that Rachel was the most important woman in Jacob's household. Ibn Ezra explains that the mention of Rachel before Leah is a recognition of which sister Jacob wanted to marry initially. He also explains *vaaseih chayil* as "acquire wealth."

ד:יב וִיהִי בֵיתְךָ כְּבֵית פֶּרֶץ אֲשֶׁר־יָלְדָה תָמָר לִיהוּדָה מִן־הַזֶּרַע אֲשֶׁר יִתֵּן יְהֹוָה לְךָ מִן־הַנַּעֲרָה הַזֹּאת:

**4:12** "And may your household be as that of Perez, whom Tamar bore to Judah through the seed that God will give you through this young woman."

By alluding to the story of Tamar (Genesis 38), the author is reminding the reader of another case of a non-Israelite woman whose children were accepted without hesitation by the Jewish community. While this may seem like a bold statement, it appears to be obvious to the author of the text. The text in Genesis does not identify Tamar as a non-Israelite. However, the text does note (Genesis 38:2) that Judah took a Canaanite woman as the mother of his sons. More importantly, such a connection relates the story and the lineage of Boaz and Ruth to the messianic line. It is more than a reference to another similar relationship.

Ruth's age is unclear at this point in the story. The author refers to her as *naarah* (literally, "a girl or youth") which we have translated as "young woman." Perhaps the author's use is more indicative of the way some people—particularly women referring to their own friends—use the term "girl" in a nonpejorative way to refer to women of any age.

To clarify the content of the verse, the *Targum* adds the words *v'hay matzlach*, "and make [your household] successful." Rashi explains the reference to Perez as it is he "from whom we have descended."

ד:יג וַיִּקַּח בֹּעַז אֶת־רוּת וַתְּהִי־לוֹ לְאִשָּׁה וַיָּבֹא אֵלֶיהָ וַיִּתֵּן יְהוָה לָהּ הֵרָיוֹן וַתֵּלֶד בֵּן:

4:13 BOAZ MARRIED RUTH AND MADE LOVE TO HER, AND GOD ALLOWED HER TO CONCEIVE AND SHE HAD A SON.

The text is more descriptive in Hebrew than the poetic English might suggest. For this reason we have translated "Boaz took Ruth as his wife" as "Boaz married Ruth." Similarly we have rendered "had intercourse with her" as "made love to her." Given what has taken place previously in Ruth's life, the role of God in her conception is important for the author to note. A literal read of the text would be "God granted her conception." Since this is a book that emphasizes the need to carry on a man's name through children, we have translated "she conceived a son" literally, as did the *Targum*. Again, given Ruth's former status as a Moabite, it is important to alleviate any lingering doubt in the reader's mind. God affirmed their relationship and even blessed them with a child, an important statement of approval from the biblical perspective.

ד:יד וַתֹּאמַרְנָה הַנָּשִׁים אֶל־נָעֳמִי בָּרוּךְ יְהוָה אֲשֶׁר לֹא הִשְׁבִּית לָךְ גֹּאֵל הַיּוֹם וְיִקָּרֵא שְׁמוֹ בְּיִשְׂרָאֵל:

4:14 THE WOMEN SAID TO NAOMI, "PRAISED IS GOD WHO TODAY HAS NOT LEFT YOU WITHOUT A REDEEMER. MAY GOD'S NAME BE CELEBRATED IN ALL ISRAEL.

It is unclear who are the women speaking. In the verse, Boaz is indicated as the redeemer, taking on the moniker previously used by the relative earlier in the story.

The *Targum* translates the text literally. Ibn Ezra uses this verse as an opportunity to remind us that the "redeemer" is the one who establishes the name of the deceased on the property that had belonged to him. Ibn Ezra's comment is insightful. He teaches that the one who acts is deserving of being named in this case as redeemer. Entitlement is insufficient. One has to earn praise through one's actions.

ד:טו וְהָיָה לָךְ לְמֵשִׁיב נֶפֶשׁ וּלְכַלְכֵּל אֶת־שֵׂיבָתֵךְ כִּי כַלָּתֵךְ אֲשֶׁר־
אֲהֵבַתֶךְ יְלָדַתּוּ אֲשֶׁר־הִיא טוֹבָה לָךְ מִשִּׁבְעָה בָּנִים:

**14:15** "HE WILL GIVE YOU A NEW LEASE ON LIFE AND WILL
TAKE CARE OF YOU IN OLD AGE. HE IS THE CHILD OF
YOUR DAUGHTER-IN-LAW, WHO LOVES YOU AND WHO
HAS BEEN BETTER TO YOU THAN SEVEN SONS."

This seems to be a continuation of the praise of Boaz in the previous verse, but is
actually a reference to Boaz and Ruth's child.

As is noted in the Koehler-Baumgartner *Lexicon* (p. 1433), *meishiv nefesh* means
"to restore liveliness, vitality; to refresh." We have translated the term in a
contemporary American idiom that provides this same sense. *L'chalkeil* comes from
the root *kol* and means "sustain." Thus, "sustain in your old age" would mean
"to take care of you in old age," rather than "to take of your old age."

Ibn Ezra reminds us of the use of *l'chalkeil* in Genesis 47:12, where the Torah tells
us that "Joseph supported his father" and his entire family and sustained them with
food during the famine.

ד:טז וַתִּקַּח נָעֳמִי אֶת־הַיֶּלֶד וַתְּשִׁתֵהוּ בְחֵיקָהּ וַתְּהִי־לוֹ לְאֹמֶנֶת:

**4:16** NAOMI TOOK THE CHILD AND HELD IT IN HER BOSOM.
SHE BECAME ITS NURSE.

While the imagery seems to suggest that Naomi served as a wet nurse to the infant, it
is more likely that she simply helped to care for it. Either way it is read, it can be
understood that Naomi was deeply connected to the child and that his birth helped
restore some happiness to her after all her misfortune.

ד:יז וַתִּקְרֶאנָה לוֹ הַשְּׁכֵנוֹת שֵׁם לֵאמֹר יֻלַּד־בֵּן לְנָעֳמִי וַתִּקְרֶאנָה שְׁמוֹ
עוֹבֵד הוּא אֲבִי־יִשַׁי אֲבִי דָוִד:

**4:17** THE NEIGHBOR WOMEN GAVE THE CHILD A NAME,
DECLARING, "A SON IS BORN TO NAOMI." THEY
CALLED HIM BY THE NAME OF OVED. HE WAS THE
FATHER OF JESSE, WHO WAS THE FATHER OF DAVID.

Given the detailed nature of the verse, the *Targum* translates it literally. However,
Ibn Ezra, picking up on the major importance of the verse, connects the birth
of Ruth's child to the eventual King David, who is thought by Jewish tradition to be

the predecessor of the Messiah. (The genealogy of David that is reported by the author in Ruth 4:18–22 is repeated in I Chronicles 2:5–15.) Yet, Ibn Ezra's major concern is with the ages of those in David's genealogy when they gave birth to their own children. While it seems like he is attempting to support the genealogical claim made in this verse and those that follow, it is possible that this is Ibn Ezra's way of conveying doubts about the entire genealogy. He maintains that 366 years passed from the time of entrance to the Land of Israel until the birth of David. This claim is based on the statement, "And it transpired in the 480th year after the Israelites came out of Egypt in the fourth year of Solomon's reign over Israel, in the month of Ziv [Iyar], the second month, that he began to build the House of God" (I Kings 6:1). He reasons that David lived to be about seventy—an assumption based on the text "He died in good old age" (1 Chronicles 29:28)—and that the Israelites wandered in the desert for forty years—but that would make the period of Joshua and the Judges only four years long. Though Ibn Ezra's comments indicate doubt regarding the relationship of Ruth to David, Jewish tradition has seen Ruth as a progenitor of the Messiah, a sign of her great righteousness.

ד:יח וְאֵלֶּה תּוֹלְדוֹת פָּרֶץ פֶּרֶץ הוֹלִיד אֶת־חֶצְרוֹן:

**4:18** THESE ARE THE GENERATIONS OF PEREZ: PEREZ FATHERED HEZRON.

Rashi explains to the reader that since previous verses in the Book of Ruth linked David to Ruth, the author must now indicate David's relationship to Judah.

ד:יט וְחֶצְרוֹן הוֹלִיד אֶת־רָם וְרָם הוֹלִיד אֶת־עַמִּינָדָב:

**4:19** HEZRON FATHERED RAM, AND RAM FATHERED AMINADAV.

Again, the *Targum* translates literally. While Rashi does not comment on the verse, Ibn Ezra continues his comment from 4:17. He concludes that all of the men in this genealogy had children at an advanced age. Support for such a view comes from Boaz's instruction to Ruth to avoid going after young men in 3:10.

וְעַמִּינָדָב הוֹלִיד אֶת־נַחְשׁוֹן וְנַחְשׁוֹן הוֹלִיד אֶת־שַׂלְמָה: **ד:כ**

**4:20** AMINADAV FATHERED NAHSHON, AND NAHSHON
FATHERED SALMAH.

This emphasis on genealogy seems to be an attempt to dispel doubt as to the connection between Ruth and the Davidic line leading to the Messiah. In its translation, the *Targum* expands the verse by adding *rav bet abba l'vayt yehudah* (head of the father's house of the House of Judah) to the identification of Nahshon and by identifying Salmah as "the righteous one of Bethlehem and Netofah (*d'batilu b'noi parzavan d'otiv Yeravam chayva al orchai*) whose sons removed the guards that wicked Jeroboam had set up to block the roads to Jerusalem so that the deeds of the father and the deeds of the son were likened to a balm." This is a wordplay on the word *netofah*, which can be understood either as the place name of Netofah or as a "balm." (See Babylonian Talmud, *Taanit* 30b and *Bava Kama* 121b.)

וְשַׂלְמוֹן הוֹלִיד אֶת־בֹּעַז וּבֹעַז הוֹלִיד אֶת־עוֹבֵד: **ד:כא**

**4:21** SALMON FATHERED BOAZ, AND BOAZ FATHERED
OVED.

This verse brings the genealogy to date, reflecting the child born in verse 13. The author seems to make a change in the name of Nahshon's child from verse 20 to verse 21. Note that Salmah and Salmon are variants of the same name. The *Targum* adds that Boaz had another name: Dozan the prince. It was by his merit, claims the *Targum*, that the Israelites were saved from their enemies. And it was because of his prayer that famine was removed from the Land of Israel. Furthermore, the *Targum* adds that Boaz's son Oved served God with a perfect heart. The *Targum* may simply be offering an explanation of his name, what is called a folk etymology, since Oved means "the one who serves; a servant." Ibn Ezra reminds the reader that both Boaz and Oved were old when they fathered children.

וְעֹבֵד הוֹלִיד אֶת־יִשָׁי וְיִשַׁי הוֹלִיד אֶת־דָּוִד: **ד:כב**

**4:22** OVED FATHERED YISHAI [JESSE], AND YISHAI [JESSE]
FATHERED DAVID.

While this verse may seem anticlimatic, it is, in fact, extremely important. This verse is the point of the entire book: a woman, previously a Moabite—forbidden to Israel—a stranger to the community, contains within her the seed to redemption. Just as the stories abound of Elijah the prophet appearing in the form of a beggar and then encouraging people to treat all beggars with warmth, the potential for redemption is contained within all newcomers to the Jewish community. Thus, it is incumbent on all of us to reach out and bring them in.

Yishai is usually transliterated as Jesse. The *Targum* expands this verse by explaining that Yishai is "called *nachash* [a reference to a snake, but it can also mean augury or copper] because there was never found in him any cause or fault that would warrant him being handed over to the Angel of Death and his soul taken from him. So he lived a very long time until God remembered the advice that *chivyah* [the snake] had given to Eve, Adam's wife, to eat of the fruit of the Tree of Knowledge of Good and Evil. Because of that advice, all who live on earth are condemned to death. For that reason, Yishai the righteous one who fathered David, king of Israel, had to die." Just as the death of our ancestors allowed us to live, so too does the death of Yishai usher in the possibility of the Messiah and redemption of the Jewish people.

## *Davidic Kingdom and Its Restoration*

David was the second king of Israel (ca. 1000–960 B.C.E.). Under David's reign the tribes of Israel were united and became a nation. One of David's crowning achievements was the capture of Jerusalem from the Jebusites. There he built a new Tabernacle to which he brought the Ark of the Covenant. Jerusalem came to be called the City of David, the heart of his kingdom and the capital of Israel. According to traditional Jewish theology, the Messiah will be a descendant of the line of David, and thus David's rule will be established once again. The Temple, too, will be rebuilt. Reform Judaism has challenged this notion and conceives of a messianic era ushered in by a generation of righteousness, rather than by one individual.

# GLEANINGS

## *Love*

A fundamental belief of Judaism holds that the intimacy, commitment, and trust we build with our human partner educates us for our relationship with God. The idea that human relationships mirror and help us forge our relationship with the divine is put forth by the prophets, especially Hosea and Jeremiah, and, if we accept the traditional interpretation, by the Song of Songs. Our experience of love and covenant is colored by Jewish folklore that extols the desirability and even divinity of marriage. (Question: What has God been doing since the Creation? Answer: Arranging marriages.) But along with familial love, the biblical text exhorts us to love our neighbor and to love even the stranger, "for you were strangers in the Land of Egypt'' (Deut. 10:19). Loving God enables us to love the stranger, because thanks to our love of God, we can feel nondefensive, safe, and generous. Loving God also leads us to love anyone God loves, however lowly (along the lines of ''love me, love my dog''). Our love for God also allows us to discover God in and through our finite human loves.

Carol Ochs, Our Lives as Torah: Finding God in Our Own Stories<br>(San Francisco: Jossey-Bass, 2001), 7–8

## The Mitzvah of Conversion

Conversion to Judaism is not for the sake of the survival of a group or for ethnic comfort. Becoming Jewish is not a matter of convenience for those born of Jewish parents. Judaism is not a matter of culinary taste, a familiar dialect or insider jokes. Conversion to Judaism is not an accommodation to the preferences of habit. In a loving conversion, the chupah is not a cover for our embarrassment within the family. The chupah is turned into a sacred canopy that covers bride and groom with the transcendent Jewish mission to reflect God's image in the world. Genuine conversion affects the native born and the Jew by choice. Conversion means that Judaism is not genes and chromosomes but a free, reasoned and passional choice. It is to fulfill the covenanted promise of our father Abraham, the first convert. Jewish mission does not mean denigration of other religions or the vulgar promotion of evangelical enthusiasm, cake and circus conversion. Jewish mission means that we act out our belief that far from being a parochial, sectarian, ethnic clan, we are a people whose faith and wisdom and ethics has endured for four millennia. To those who thirst we declare with the prophet Isaiah: ''Ho everyone that thirsteth come to the waters— even he that hath no money—bring wine and milk and drink.''

Harold Schulweis, ''The Mitzvah of Conversion,'' Rabbi Harold Schulweis Archives,<br>Valley Beth Shalom, Encino, CA, p. 5, http://www.vbs.org/rabbi/hshulw/convert_bot.htm

## The Human Role in Redemption

The Jewish tradition teaches us that *mashiach* [messiah] arises from Israel. Whether we say Messiah or Messianic Age, *mashiach* or *y'mot hamashiach* [days of the Messiah, or Messianic Age], do we believe that a time of justice and peace for all humanity arises uniquely from the Jewish people? What specific role does the Jewish people play in the messianic process? Franz Rosenzweig believed that the Jewish people has a unique responsibility to keep the lamp burning, to live in its particularism. History does not belong to Judaism, he said, it belongs to Christianity. The end of history, however, belongs to Judaism. Christianity and, therefore, the world are moving to the place where Judaism already is. Even now, if the Jews were to disappear, Christianity would descend into paganism. Judaism and the Jewish people are essential for redemption. It is our unique responsibility to continue to be what we are.

Perhaps the Jewish people has a special mandate through our prophetic heritage to work for social justice. Can we really say that Jews have a greater obligation than the rest of humanity to be moral? Is this not a human obligation? How can our particularity consist in doing what every human being should do? It is difficult to believe that Judaism teaches that Jews have a stronger obligation than all others to be ethical; surely we call upon all humanity to strive for justice.

Perhaps what is unique is not our obligation to be ethical, but our teaching that the center of religion is ethics; it is our particular message for the world that justifies our particular existence. If we examine the historical record, is it not true that only religions that grow out of Torah—Judaism, Christianity, and Islam—have a concept of this-worldly redemption? Does any culture or philosophy not based on the Torah, for example, that of ancient Greece, have any concept of repentance—a necessary component of ethical activism—or historical change, or messianism? Perhaps, indeed, the message of Torah is unique. . . . Even though most of the world accepts the message of Isaiah that "nation shall not lift up sword against nation, neither shall they continue to learn the arts of war," still the purpose of the Jewish people on earth has not been fulfilled. Our people's particularity, our awesome history, our very existence are mysterious and we do fulfill a purpose by keeping the lamp burning.

Michael S. Stroh, "Mending the World and the Evil Inclination: The Human Role in Redemption,"<br>in *Duties of the Soul: The Role of the Commandments in Liberal Judaism*,<br>ed. Niles E. Goldstein and Peter S. Knobel (New York: UAHC Press, 1999), 90–91

## The Perils of Jewish Messianism

Jews have been able to keep going because we refuse to believe that our destiny is an endless repetition of defeats and disasters, a human treadmill from which we can never exit. Central to Jewish belief is the conviction that Jews will be around to experience the miracles and wonders of the coming of the Messiah. It is this hope that has given us the courage to continue. But Jewish messianism also has a destructive side, a mutant strain, that arises in times of upheaval. It strikes whenever apocalyptic Jewish movements have acted to hasten the coming of the Messiah. The result, almost always, has been fierce factionalism and violence. . . .

The earliest evidence of Jewish belief in messianic redemption can be traced in the Bible to the tumultuous period following the death of King Solomon and the subsequent destruction of the two successor kingdoms—Israel in the north (722 B.C.E.) and Judea in the south (586 B.C.E.) While Judea was still independent, the Prophet Isaiah had seen the ecstatic vision of a "descendant of the house of Jesse"

(Isaiah 11:1), an heir of the Jewish royal line, who would lead his people, and the world, toward a time of peace "when the lion would lie down with the lamb."

... When will the Messiah come? In Sanhedrin 97b it is written that any Jew who claims to have figured out the time of the "end of days" will be punished with a short life. Perhaps the most Jewish answer to this question was given by the twentieth-century Israeli scholar Yeshayahu Leibowitz, who said: the Messiah who appears and announces himself is always a false Messiah. We do not know what guise the Messiah may take, and we cannot force him to arrive to suit our will or needs. As humans we have it within our control to effect only one contribution in helping redeem the world: to work for more justice and more decency so that we humans will survive our capacity for self-destruction.

Rabbi Arthur Hertzberg, "Storming Heaven: The Perils of Jewish Messianism,"
*Reform Judaism* 27, no. 4 (Summer 1999): 10, 12, 17

# *Biographies*

**Rabbi Allan L. Berkowitz** does his outreach work in San Jose, California. His interest in social action led him to found San Jose's Tikkun Bayit, the "Community Peace Corps," which links volunteers with projects in ethnically diverse neighborhoods.

**Shoshana Brown** serves as cantor at Kehillath Shalom Synagogue in Cold Spring Harbor, New York.

**Rabbi Rachel Cowan** is director of the Spirituality Institute in New York City. With her late husband, Paul, she wrote *Mixed Blessings: Marriages between Jews and Christians*.

**Anita Diamant** is the author of a number of popular books, including *The New Jewish Wedding*, *Living a Jewish Life*, and the runaway best seller *The Red Tent*, a novel. She lives in Newton, Massachusetts.

**Rabbi Laura Geller** is senior rabbi of Temple Emanu-El in Beverly Hills, California.

**Rabbi Daniel Gordis** is director of the Mandel Fellows Program and a member of the senior staff of the Mandel Foundation, Sector on Jewish Education and Continuity, based in Jerusalem. He is also the author of numerous books, including *If a Place Can Make You Cry: Dispatches from an Anxious State* and *God Was Not in the Fire: The Search for a Spiritual Judaism*.

**Joel Lurie Grishaver** is the creative chairperson of Torah Aura Productions and the Alef Design Group. He is a faculty member of the Department of Continuing Education of the University of Judaism and a consultant to the Whizin Institute for Jewish Family Living. Joel is the author of more than fifty books, including *Learning Torah*, *Shema Is for Real*, *And You Shall Be a Blessing*, and *40 Things You Can Do to Save the Jewish People*.

**Rabbi Arthur Hertzberg** is Bronfman Visiting Professor of the Humanities at New York University and the author of ten books, including *The Zionist Idea*.

**Rabbi Margaret Holub** is the spiritual leader of a rural, alternative "shtetl" on the North Coast of California.

**Rabbi Lawrence Kushner** is the scholar-in-residence at Congregation Emanu-El in San Francisco. Most recently, he was rabbi-in-residence at Hebrew Union College–Jewish Institute of Religion, New York. Rabbi Kushner served as spiritual leader of Congregation Beth El of Sudbury, Massachusetts, for twenty-five years and is the author of numerous books and articles, including *God Was in This Place and I, i Did Not Know*.

**Rabbi Jane Rachel Litman** is co-editor of *Lifecyles: Jewish Women on Biblical Themes in Contemporary Life,* volume 2. She is also the rabbi educator at Congregation Beth El of Berkeley, California.

**Deborah Dash Moore** is an American Jewish historian and the author/editor of numerous books in the field, including the two-volume *Jewish Women in America: An Historical Encyclopedia*. She is professor of religion at Vassar College.

**Patti Moskovitz** has been a Jewish educator for over forty years. For more than fifteen years, she has been engaged in instructing candidates for conversion to Judaism. She also teaches Judaism to many interfaith couples who seek to learn more about Jewish tradition.

**Dr. Carol Ochs** is director of the Graduate Studies Program at Hebrew Union College–Jewish Institute of Religion, New York, where she is also visiting professor of philosophy. She is the author of numerous works on spirituality, including *Jewish Spiritual Guidance* (with Kerry Olitzky) and *Reaching Godward: Voices from Jewish Spiritual Guidance*.

**Susan Weidman Schneider** is the editor of the Jewish feminist quarterly *Lilith* and the author of *Jewish and Female*.

**Rabbi Harold M. Schulweis** is the senior rabbi of Valley Beth Shalom in Encino, California. He is the founder of the Jewish Foundation for Rescuers and the author of *For Those Who Can't Believe* and *Finding Each Other in Judaism*.

**Rabbi Michael S. Stroh** is the rabbi of Temple Har Zion in Toronto. He served as president of ARZA Canada and was an instructor at Queens College of the City University of New York and the University of Waterloo. He also taught at the School of Sacred Music and the School of Education, Hebrew Union College–Jewish Institute of Religion, New York.